requiem for the toad

requiem for the toad

selected poems of
gerald locklin

edited by
clint margrave

Books™

The New York Quarterly Foundation, Inc.
Beacon, New York

NYQ Books™ is an imprint of The New York Quarterly Foundation, Inc.

The New York Quarterly Foundation, Inc.
P. O. Box 470
Beacon, NY 12508

www.nyq.org

First Edition

Set in New Baskerville

Layout by Raymond Hammond

Cover Design by Clint Margrave

Cover Art by Ray Zepeda

Library of Congress Control Number: 2023952457

ISBN: 978-1-63045-103-5

requiem for the toad

CONTENTS

Introduction xiv
Editor's Note xvii

Rainy Season 19
The Toad 20
Beer 21
poop 23
the hook shot 24
pedagogy 26
a later poem for maureen 27
my-six-year-old 28
Peanuts 29
Friday: 3 p.m. 31
death of a lawnmower 32
california 33
captain midnight cowboy sister carrie 35
Tap Dancing Lessons 38
the sort of thing you just don't need to face 39
Don't Rest on Your Laurels 40
Transcendent Logic 43
Where Has Love Gone? 44
Bill 45
a guide to the cinema 47
requiem for three bar guys 48
New York Punks and California Studs 51
Two for the Seesaw and One for the Road 52
Illumination 53
Divorcee 54
at 37 55

Love Story 56
Wynken, Blynken 58
I Wish They All Could Be California Girls 59
The Death of Jean-Paul Sartre 60
On Violence: A Note to Reviewers 63
Patriotic Poem 64
the best year of her life 65
shit 66
Character Witness 67
I Do Belong to the American Federation of Labor! 68
Mindlessness Over Matter 69
It Takes, It Takes a Busy Man 71
The Age of Antibiotics 72
Shoes to Fill, or Don't Make Me Laugh 73
The Walden/Woodstock Apartments 74
RIVERRUN PAST DICK AND JANE 75
Homage to John Cage 76
No Rush 77
an uncool yul 78
the freedom fighters 80
a constituency of dunces 81
minimal affirmation 82
On the Rack 83
found poem 84
my mother's funeral 85
st. francis would have approved 89
ancient math 90
From a Usually Reliable Source 91
At the University College of North Wales at Bangor 92

You, Gail Sheehy 93

el amor brujo 94

mannequin 95

the woman i'm going out with believes in god 96

my kinda guy 97

what i learned from watching the pink panther cartoon festival 98

my six-month old daughter 99

shadows 100

he need regret nothing 101

Old Nassau's Black Sheep 103

my daughter and the firebird 104

I've Always Enjoyed Her Sense of Humor 106

Why I Go to Art Exhibits 107

Open Admissions 108

The New Kids on the Quad 109

on the death of a great comedian, spring 1994 110

The New Male 112

Political Poems 113

The Last Round-Up 114

I Am Not Gerald Locklin 116

Sartre Misunderstood 118

Good Neighbor Pete 119

David Hockney: *My Bedroom* 120

David Hockney: *De Longpre Avenue*, 1976 121

To Get What You Pay for Is The Best You Can Expect 122

Summer School 124

The Bunnyfish 126

I'm about Ready for the Venerable Bede 128

an easy-going weekend 129

hot sunday afternoon 130
Where Have You Gone, T.S. Eliot? 131
none too soon 132
The Nurses 133
Obviously Not a Gambler 135
Toad's Handicap 136
Placing the Blame 137
Running into Ger 139
The Witnesses Meet My Teenage Daughter 140
An Immortal in the Flesh 142
Personal Storage 144
give me a break 145
when the drinking was good 146
Un Bel Di 150
The Iceberg Theory 151
where we are (for edward field) 152
One to Whom It Is Not a Joking Matter 153
The Condemned Man's Last Supper 155
rejection slips and slip-ups 156
Where's Wally? 157
Jocasta 158
almond blossom 159
Van Gogh Died Childless 160
Smoking Skulls II 163
Roofs in Paris 164
Deconstruction, Decentering, Demythologizing 166
No Longer A Teenager 167
Happiness 169
Was Charles Bukowski a Better Writer
than William Shakespeare? 170

everyone lives a lie 171

the loser 173

forget the sexual politics 174

amedeo modigliani: reverdy, cendrars, et cetera 175

amedeo modigliani: *pencil portrait of hans arp,* 1916 176

amedeo modigliani: *seated nude with folded hands,* 1918 177

men are from mars; women are from bellevue 178

the conqueror 179

enzo cucchi: *i uno* 180

paul klee: *this star teaches bending* 181

the ultimate pessimist 182

henry's gift 183

Don't Ask Us to Plan too Far Ahead 185

ivan albright: *into the world there came a soul called ida,* 1929-30 186

a streetcar named greed 187

his mother dressed him as a girl 188

eastern guys appreciate their wives more 190

you fit in eventually 191

as time goes by 193

reprieve 194

My Three Sons 195

Vincent Van Gogh: *The Mulberry Tree,* 1889 196

Strong Women 197

Second-Hand Television 198

Milestones 199

The Firmament 200

Cathedral 201

Henri de Toulouse-Lautrec: *profile of a prostitute,* 1892-94 204

the stepford boys 205
Wedlock Sunday 206
Gerry's Day 207
Not on the Church Calendar 209
Colonoscopy 210
Diane Arbus: *42nd Street Movie Theatre Audience* 212
Cézanne: *The Artist's Father* 213
The Ungrateful Dead 214
For Henry Denander 215
Madonna and Child, Sculpture, Italy, 1125-1150 216
Vanessa Bell: *Charleston Garden,* 1933 217
Good in Bed 219
Pierre Auguste Renoir 220
Why I Didn't Make the Rounds 221
God Needs More Churches 222
Can't Buy You Love 223
I Hate Hollywood 224
Thumbnail Guide for the Senior Couplers 226
timing is everything 227
Olfactory Poetics 228
No Free Lunch 229
the common reader 230
Matisse: *Le Bonheur de Vivre,* 1905-06 232
albrecht dürer: *adam and eve,* 1504 233
My Fifteen Seconds of Fame 234
the silence 235
at midnight 236

Acknowledgments 238

INTRODUCTION

"if i don't write their requiem /who the fuck do you know that will?" says Gerald Locklin in his poem, "requiem for three bar guys."

Poets are not just the recorders of their own lives, but of others' lives, of moments lost to time, of ideas, memories, experiences, emotion. Neither report nor history, a poet's record is not literal though it may be concerned with what's real, not factual though always concerned with what's true. A poet takes the raw stuff of life and shapes it into meaning, then gives it back to the world. And when a poet dies, he doesn't really die, but leaves us with a body of work that remains alive.

There are over 3000 poems in Locklin's repertoire. Having spent the past year and a half reading most of them—an overwhelming task simply by its sheer volume—there is nearly a poem about everything and everyone (I even surprisingly found one where I get a mention). And though we should never assume that poet and speaker, or poet and his amphibious persona, Toad, are one and the same, Locklin writes with candor that at times must have brought him trouble in his personal life, but which, as a writer, he remained committed to at all costs. The same people, places, and things that filled up Gerry's life, also fill up his poems, including his children, writing, women (wives and others), drinking (in the early decades), not drinking (in the later decades), teaching, students, food, art, literature, jazz, and sports. But the main subject remains the poet himself, in all his hilarious, absurd, and often divulging ways. Reading Locklin, one understands that he revealed the most about himself before he ever gave himself permission to write about anyone else.

One might say his poems are also a requiem for a time and place, mostly Southern California except for those poems about traveling, and specifically Long Beach, CA through the 70s, 80s, 90s, 2000s. But they are much more than that. They are a record of all that it means to be human, to have laughed, to have loved, to have fucked, and to have lived a deliberate, free, and authentic life.

For 40 years, Gerry also worked as a professor at California State University, Long Beach and never apologized for it, even when being a poet who worked in academia became unpopular in some of his friendship circles (see Bukowski). He never felt the need to pretend to be anything other than who he was. One had to work, after all. The starving artist was a romantic myth for the very young and naïve, as was the idea that a poet could earn a living by writing poetry. And there was no shame in being a teacher. It was an honorable job with a lot of vacation time to write, even if Gerry found himself often stuck between two worlds, at odds with the stuffiness and conformity of academia, and yet perhaps, too academic for the street poets. As John Penner said of him in the *LA Times*, he was "a rebel among academics and an academic among rebels."

In a sense, Gerry was an everyman, though I hesitate to use that term, because he was also like no one else. Still, he believed in the decent everyday people of this planet and he never condescended towards them, unlike some of his academic and artistic counterparts. Gerry was anything but a snob, and his beliefs about poetry were just as down to earth. Poetry is something for everybody and not just literature PhDs sitting in their ivory towers. Despite that he himself held a PhD, Gerry's only ivory tower in those early years was a stool at the 49rs Tavern or maybe the Reno Room in Long Beach, hanging with the regulars, who loved to harass him about the ease of his professorial life, as in this passage from his poem, "I Do Belong to the American Federation of Labor:"

> i'm sitting in the tavern
> with some of my fellow sports fans,
> all of whom are laborers,
> and someone complains that there's nothing
> to bet on in the spring
> (except for suckering an occasional greenhorn
> into a wager on the superstars competition)
>
> and i say, without thinking, "at least it's a good
>   time
> to get a little work done,"
> and Old Jim snorts, "work! you've never done
> an honest day's work, Locklin, in your goddamn life!"

Gerry believed in a poetry for people who pay rent, that could be written in a common language anyone could understand. A poetry that wasn't about displaying how clever the poet was (though he was clever), or baiting the critics with its complexities (though he was complex), but could be accessible (without insulting anyone's intelligence), humorous, entertaining, a poetry that didn't "bore the shit" out of the reader, as he so aptly puts it in one of his most iconic poems, "The Iceberg Theory." Poetry need not be dull or bleak either, even when its subject matter is serious, because one still has to find the beauty and laughter in life's absurdity.

He brought this same kind of energy to his poetry readings. A poetry reading, believe it or not, could be fun, and not drive away its audience. A poetry reading could be an event where people who were not poets could enjoy themselves, have a good laugh, or at the very least, be entertained. Gerry loved to sing and dance at his readings, even though he could do neither, which is what made it so funny.

At times, his humor could seem cynical, though he was not "the ultimate pessimist" he may have claimed to be, despite the irony of giving this title to both a poem and chapbook. He knew his cup was more full than empty. As he remarks in another poem, "at midnight," he loved life despite its struggles:

> "...for the first time in my life
> i understand why anyone would want
> to believe in reincarnation,
> and would want to come back
> to this world."

Gerry need not be reincarnated. He hasn't left this world. With over 3000 poems, 150 books, multiple short stories, novels, essays, and forty years of teaching and inspiring thousands of students, Gerry doesn't need anyone to write his requiem.

Clint Margrave
Long Beach, CA

EDITOR'S NOTE:

Gerry had an idiosyncratic way of sometimes using lower case punctuation in his poems and sometimes not. His friend Patricia Cherin refers to this as different "case moods," depending on whether he wanted to be more "iconoclast or classic." The consensus around his use of lower case seems to be that it was both an homage to and influenced by e e cummings. I suppose an academic somewhere can study this more thoroughly someday. As the editor of this collection, I tried my best to find and honor the "case moods" based on the poems' original publications. With such a large volume of work, the task could be overwhelming at times and incomplete, but I tried my best to honor his legacy.

requiem for the toad

Rainy Season

The old woman at the window,
gray as vinegar and vicious
as a cracked windowpane,
says nary a word.

But the great gray spider
out in the rain
understands.
All our webs get wet in the spring.

The Toad

"Do you love me?" I asked.
"Love you? How could I love a toad?"

That made a lot of sense,
so I asked her, "How's about
if we just kind of sleep together?"
Naturally she had to think that one over at some length:

"And never turn on the lights?"
"All right," I said.
"And you are gone before the sun comes up?"
"All right," I said.
She lowered her voice: "But you will
love me toad-style, not like humans?"
"How else?" I said.

"Well then," she said, "we'll try it
for a week, but let's not ask for miracles."

I came to her each night for half a year,
returning with the sun to quarry
in the streaming, mud-caked bean fields.
Did she ever think about me at her
gay martini lunches, her dinners
for two at Scandia?
To think I, a humble toad,
had given my heart to a fashion designer!

In May I lost her to a troll,
a recent arrival from Brooklyn.

Beer

It takes a lot to get you there, but it won't
    kill you either.

Kids like it. The foam makes a fine mustache.
    When they go to sleep they dream of goofy
    pink dragons and slippery little smiling
    fish.

To the adolescent it is the first taste of the
    earth's bitterness. He has to pretend it gets him high.
    He is afraid it will give him zits, and maybe it will.
    He gives it to his girl and thinks it is because of it
    she gives herself to him.

She doesn't like the taste of it and never will.
    She doesn't have the thirst for it. She
    is afraid it will give her a gut, and
    maybe it will. Eventually she'll be a
    little insulted when it's offered her.
    And probably should be.

But the best of friendships are formed over
    it. It helps men to speak to each other,
    a difficult thing these days. It lets
    men sing without embarrassment of auld
    lang syne and of the sheep that went astray
    somewhere along the line. It goes excellently
    with pool and pickled eggs, beef jerky and
    baseball games. Contrary to popular opinion,
    it is good for the kidneys, affords them exercise.
    It is good for all the appetites.

We all go beyond it; we always come back to it.
   It is the friend who eases us through
   our philosophies. It is the friend we talk
   to about our women, the one who agrees
   with us that they are not all that
   important. It restores our courage in the
   face of cowardly sobrieties. It laughs
   with us at our most serious poems, weeps
   at our pratfalls. It remembers us; it
   takes us back.

Finally, this blessed beer, it eases us towards
   sleep.

poop

my daughter, blake, is in kindergarten. they are teaching her to be a docile
   citizen and, incidentally to read, concurrently, like many of us, she
   has become a trifle anal compulsive, complications ensue.

i ask her what she has learned today. she says, "i learned the pledge of
   allegiance." "how does it go?" i ask. "it goes," she says, "i poop
   allegiance to the poop of the united poops of ameripoop."

"that's good," i say, "that's very good. what else?" "o say can you poop,
   by the dawn's early poop, what so proudly we pooped…"

for christmas, she improvises "away in a pooper, all covered with poop, the
   little lord poopus lay pooping his poop."

she has personalized other traditional favorites as well. someone, perhaps
   her grandmother, tried to teach her the "our father." her version goes,
   "our pooper, who art in poopland, hallowed be thy poop, thy poopdom
   poop, thy poop be pooped, on earth as it is in poopland."

surely hemingway would feel one-upped. surely the second pooping is at hand.

a fortune teller told us blake would be our greatest sorrow and our greatest
   joy. already, it is true.

the hook shot

at one time basketball was my life.
no one taught me more about the game
than don garland, my eighth grade coach.
he was a big man, firm and gentle;

only his patience exceeded the bulk
of his forearms. i never knew him to
raise his voice—but who had the
cojones to test him? he was the man.

he drilled me nightly in the hook shot:
bounce pass, step to the basket, lean
with the shoulder, brace with the elbow,
sight the glass target, and arc it up lightly.

over and over, a couple hundred
hook shots at night, but i loved it,
and i mastered it, and we won
the diocesan tournament.

you drilled me well, mr. garland;
nothing is more a part of me than my hook shot.
when i can't sleep at night,
i count hook-shots, not sheep.

and how i wish you had been my mentor
in other skills as well, like writing
and fucking and lying and being a father,

but i'm not sure how many of these
were really up your alley.
still, would that the quatrain
were as second-nature as the hook shot.

even now, on those rare occasions
when i get down to the outdoor courts,
it's nice to have the hook shot going for me;
it's about all i have left.

one last thing: i can still picture your face.
i have almost no visual imagination;
i can't for instance remember what my first wife looked like,
but i can still picture your stepping towards me,

feeding me a bounce pass. i hope your life
(like mine) has had its moments.

pedagogy

in sixth grade they gave us a belgian nun.
she was just learning the language, and she often
had to ask the English word for something.
little things like doorknobs, blackboard, chalk.

we were a rotten and sadistic bunch.
we gloried in sabotage.
our previous teacher was now in r-wing of the local
                                                hospital,
which is where you went when you couldn't stop screaming.

one day sister bonita asked us what you call
an electric outlet—you know, the thing on the wall
that you plug the plug into.
we told her it was called a cunt.

she left the room to find the janitor, to explain
what it was of hers that needed fixing, what it was
exactly that she couldn't fit the plug into.
she returned to class a tearful but a wiser woman.

which reminds me of a piece of profound advice
imparted to me by a young professor upon the occasion
of my going forth from graduate school:
"remember, locklin," he said, his hand upon my tweedy
                                                shoulder,
"in teaching you are always dealing with the criminal
                                                mentality."

a later poem for maureen

i've been obsessed with it of late,
that picture of maureen, our love-child in her arms,
she still upon the operating table,
slightly dopey, but relieved of pain,

transfigured.
they took a snapshot of her,
and her face was clean and sharp and radiant;
it shone a rodent innocence.

mo, life is not as clean and sharp
as your smile in that radiant instant;
still, how did i make it go away,
that unifying flash?

my-six-year-old

i take my daughter out to lunch.
she reads the wine list
and remembers fine points of oenology.
she inquires about the function

of the cork and soon has mastered
the fermentation process from the grape
to vinegar. she's sensible in ordering
and takes an interest in cuisine.

in fact she's about the only member of
the gentler (sic) sex whose conversation i enjoy.
for one thing she may be the only girl i know
possessed of a genuine intellectual curiosity.

and she escapes the tyranny of the obvious.
if we are dining at el matador, and i explain
the principle of corrida, she doesn't
take the side of the goddam bull.

she doesn't tell me i shouldn't drink so much.
she doesn't want to marry me.
she doesn't regale me with anecdotes of the office,
memorabilia of the student cafeteria.

she asks about paris; she asks about rome.
she finds the world funny; she finds its words
wonderful. we love each other.
i think i'll go see her right now.

Peanuts

Someday Snoopy will be dead.

Have you thought of that?

He will perhaps roll off his doghouse roof
      in the midst of some ridiculous *Luftwaffe*
      nightmare and crack his canine cranium.
      Perhaps his legions of dog germs will turn
      inexplicably upon him, a betrayal by one's own
      bacteria. His kidneys may go...or his liver
      ...or his pancreas...or his lungs. His
      brain may go, in which case he will have to spend
      his last humiliating years at the State Institution
      for Exceptional Dogs. His heart may break with
      frustration at his chronic ability to down
      the Red Baron...or to play shortstop for
      the Yankees...or to find a true love.
      Or he will come to the realization that he is,
      after all, only a dog, and that dogs do not
      live forever.

Whatever. The point is that someday Snoopy will be dead.

Charley Brown will grow up to be a successful CPA. He will
      probably also become a Governor. If so, he will behave
      with tyrannical cruelty, for there is an abiding
      bitterness within him towards his supercilious
      playmates. Given a little power, Charley Brown
      will prove to be a man obsessed with vengeance.

Lucy will grow up to be a dyke. For a while she will war
      against her bulldykedom, trying to convince herself
      that what she really needs is children. She will marry
      a nice young violinist and make him exceptionally
      miserable. They will not have any children.
      Eventually, she will give in to her origins, take a
      Ph.D. in sociology from Illinois, and, for their own
      good, grade her students on the curve.

Schroeder will never make it to Carnegie Hall. At best,
      he will be a Liberace; at worst, a cocktail pianist
      in Alhambra, California.

They will take the blanket away from Linus when he goes
      away to college. He will be a jack-off for the rest of
      his life.

Peppermint Pattie will lose her freckles, develop a bosom,
      make it big in Hollywood. She will have eight
      husbands, appear regularly on the Johnny Carson
      show, and be the least unhappy of the bunch.

All will on occasion indulge themselves in nostalgia for good
      old Snoopy. When drunk, they will tell themselves
      (and anyone else who is willing to listen) that he is
      still gunning for the Red Baron, in some great Doggie
      Heaven in the sky.

I'd like to believe that too.

Sure I would.

Friday: 3 p.m.

"It rests me to be among beautiful women." –Ezra Pound

All the sad young coeds sleepwalk
on the sands of time, no time on their hands,
but unawake they walk in lovely like
the day and talk in nonsense like the night.

I have seen the sad young coeds dreaming
through the dull classes and on sunny sundays
driving young men mad by seeming not to
care for sports cars, not to crave pastels of one

day's unreality. They are real
as short red skirts, red polished nails, crossed
legs, espresso hair, a generation lost
and found as new as new year's eve, they feel

the surf at Santa Monica is sacred,
sex does not excite them, fond
of fate, they pay lip service to dead gods
and in eternity discern a grain of sand.

All the sad young coeds arabesque
across the granite campus, high with
dissonance and dying with the risk of
living high. Let me share their joy.

31

death of a lawnmower

i am a toad;
consequently poets are forever trying
to run over me with their power mowers,
presumably so they will have
something to write about.

one tried yesterday,
but i sprang a little surprise on him:
i ate his foot off;
then i ate the lawnmower.

i'm curious to see how he will work that one
into his alexandrine strophies.

california

what the hell am i doing anyway?
i mean, my eyes are photo-sensitive,
i'm scared of big waves, and sweating in the sand
bored the knickers off me. furthermore,

i am not exactly mr. abdominal
definition of southern california.
i compensate, however, by being mr.
inarticulate (what do you say

to these blithely dispirited bodies, when
you can't tell whether they're fifteen or
thirty-five and, back home, even the ugly ones
cried rape if you so much as tipped your cap?).

of course, the beach has its moments, like parked
above the phosphorescent scaly tide
at sunset, and the girl will blossom soon,
her nipples gone dusk red, into a young woman.

even here, though, peril. only once i
tried to make it on the shore, and it
was sand up in her crotch, my crevices,
a cold wind howling at my asshole, my

corrugated knees kept sliding out
from under me, and then i lost my glasses
and my credit cards, scuttling like t.s. eliot
in flotsam and jetsam, whichever is which

never again. nor disneyland either,
although it was free and with the girl i love.
the lines are long, the rides aren't scary, people
seem to think they have fun, like

when the whole country jerked off over the moonshot.
no, and I don't want to go to marineland,
let alone busch gardens or universal stupidos.
for all of me, the queen mary could sink.

i do like rooting for the rams though, and
the lakers; i like a big league town.
and the girls don't have legs like farmers,
and it *is* the biggest ocean.

the food is the worst imaginable,
but there are all kinds of movies playing.
there are curiosities like gay bars;
might as well be where it happens first.

well, the discussion is no doubt academic,
since we're all dying of emphysema.
as grandma always used to say: you made
your oyster bed, now grovel in it.

captain midnight cowboy sister carrie

shit or shitless, as the case may be,
i'm oh so scared of ending up a derelict,
like ratso—coughing, puking, never
getting laid, shivering, falling down

the stairs, then not quite making it to
florida, a whole new start as rico.
RICO, no more ratso bullshit, *enrico*
salvatore *rizzo*, dreams dreams,

joe buck as his lever, 'cause you gotta
have a little leverage, a little something
someone needs. like talent, property,
or a big stiff texas longhorn dick,

otherwise you'll get evicted every time
you fart, and what sawbones' gonna take
time out from golf to fix your leg, what dolly's
gonna be seen with you, you pitiful pariah...

the same with dreiser's hurstwood—he loses his
leverage, in his case a white-collar job,
and after that it's the old quicksand trick,
with vicious whirlpools, like you can't get a

decent job because your clothes are wrinkled. but
you can't afford to have your pants pressed
because you're out of a job, soon you
notice your sweetheart losing interest, the bitch

you did it all for in the first place, so
you try to knock over a liquor store, but you
get shot in the balls and three-to-thirty
years besides, and meanwhile she is laying

all the mod squad who can buy her supergrass
and take her sailing off balboa,
and you get the lead in the cellblock summer play:
dryden's *all for love: or a world well lost*...

now i didn't grow up hungry and i've always had
a lever, but there've been lean times,
no car, no television set, no record player,
no beer money, no extra cash for philandering,

and i, who weigh two hundred thirty pounds,
was once down to a hundred seventy, no
money for doctors, for dentists, for books
or stamps or movies or parties or a lawyer,

always knew, though, it was temporary,
always had a lever up my sleeve, but what
if they wouldn't let me teach anymore, and i
don't make any money writing and everyone

agrees i'm not much good at anything else (if joe buck
couldn't make it as a stud, that leaves me out)
and strange girls are afraid of my long hair and
big nose, and i get surly when i get depressed...

on the way to westwood to the flick, bobbie says
"can we be rich someday," and i say, "sure,"
and she says, "can we go springtime in paris,
moonlight in vermont, autumn in new York..."

and i say, "sure," but how will i make any money
when i can't sit still for anything i can't write
in a sitting, and i won't do anything specifically
for money anyway. the paper doesn't even pay for my reviews.

and money, I guess, does matter. she says it doesn't
but she's beautiful and should be seen by men
around the world (and so should my wife who is beautiful
and young and never gets out except to the laundry…)

after the show, we go to santa monica
for fish and chips, but i'm caught short and have
to borrow a couple of bucks from her. we drive
the coast of malibu and think about a motel.

but that would truly be an extravagance.
the forty miles back we wonder whether i
can get her on the payroll as student assistant.
this morning, at home, i find the rent-check has bounced.
                    envoi

i'm almost thirty and my lawyer says it's a critical
age for poets and that i should see a shrink
but my head is straight since bobbie, i'll just
go easy on the booze, and stay away from the parabolic

naturalistic novels. instead i'll re-read
gatsby, which will remind me that money
is shit and that those who love it are shitless,
and up my sleeve i'll keep the level mind.

Tap Dancing Lessons

back in the second grade
my mother had a brainstorm,
she would sturdy up my spindly legs
with dancing lessons at marge miller's studio.

i had my choice of tap or ballet
and instinctively i chose tap,
not so much because i had anything against homosexuality
as that I sensed the rise of ed sullivan, and the whole third world.

i quit dancing two years later
so as not to miss the notre dame broadcasts,
just as many years later i was to be spared a life of shame
when i quit the boy scouts to watch i love lucy.

the funny thing is, my mother's crazy idea worked.
it worked so well that for years i moved around
with the shape of a wigwam, a sort of winnebago teepee—
picture if you can a six-foot dwarf.

only years of lifting weights and drinking beer
have given me any semblance of an upper body,
and even that, like a glacier succumbing to the centuries,
is sloping badly towards the equatorial belt.

still, i was better at it than you might imagine.
mrs. miller once informed my mother that i was
her "little fred astaire." and even now, at parties,
i am apt to break into my "shuffle-off-to-buffalo."

i have two other steps in my repertoire:
the "bell step," although i barely leave the floor now,
and the old standby "stamp-shuffle-ball-change."
the cossack squat" is just a memory.

the sort of thing you just don't need to face

It was the morning after the Christmas party
and I was circling towards the liquor store
when I passed the automatic news vending machine.

The headline read: DARWIN OBLITERATED.

Oh my God, I thought, some prick
has gone and refuted
the theory of natural selection
while I was too drunk to defend it.

It was only hours later,
hearing on the news about the Australian cyclone,

that my philosophical foundations were restored.

Don't Rest on Your Laurels

God, I couldn't begin to count
how many times I heard that phrase as a kid.

It was a favorite of my father.
When he'd discern me lingering a bit too rosily
in the afterglow of some minor achievement,
he would swiftly endeavor to rescue me
from the jaws of complacency:

"You have every right to be proud of yourself...
BUT DON'T REST ON YOUR LAURELS!"

It's a funny phrase actually—so Grecian and semipoetic
—so unlike my poems,
which he probably wouldn't consider much
of an accomplishment anyway—
my mother certainly doesn't—
though, who knows, he might surprise me,
he died before I began to publish,
and he'd always gone along with everything else
I perpetrated.

Another funny thing, though,
is that he had no laurels, in the common usage,
to rest upon himself.
Please please please,
don't think I'm putting him down for that.
I went without nothing.
He suffered my mother for my sake.
Most importantly, he always made it clear to me
that I was loved by him.

He was the most lovable man I ever knew.
All my aunts envied my mother.
Men with fingernails that would never come clean

wept at his funeral.
I wept for three days running
and have not altogether stopped.

In truth, however, he had never striven for fame
or money or creative excellence or a much better job
or anything else that one would ordinarily associate
with "laurels."
I don't mean that he didn't work hard.
He worked much harder than I can imagine
(much harder, it goes without saying, than I do)
and, a handyman, he did a lot for others in his off-hours.

But he did sit around his share also—
at ballgames and Sunday family dinners
and in the bars with his friends
and on Monday night with me,
playing chess and watching *I Love Lucy*
and Brian Donleavy in *Foreign Intrigue*.
He sipped Imperial Blend backed by water.

No, listen, please understand,
I'm not putting him down for that.
I wish I were sitting in his lap right now.

And I realize that by the time I knew him
he had come back from the war,
a man weakened by diabetes,

and I know that his advice was sound.
I know that people when they retire, for instance,
have a tendency to die,
and you don't have to travel far to find examples
of people who are resting, not even on their laurels,
but solidly on the seat of their pants.

Still, why, when I spend a few hours with my kids,
should I find myself asking,
"Is this another insidious way of resting on one's laurels?"

Old man,
(which is what I think we called each other)
I realize that I teach shamelessly few hours
and that I have some of my summers off,

but still
sometimes I think I need a rest.

Transcendent Logic

after the film, my little boy,
who now must cope with a divorce
as well as the even more terrifying realization
that he will never catch up in age with his sister,

grows strangely quiet.

"what's the matter, big guy?" i ask.

"nothing," he says.

"come on," i urge, *"something's wrong."*

"if something's wrong," he says,
"please tell me what it is."

at a loss of words,
i once again fail him.

Where Has Love Gone?

Something has gone out of our romance, love:
we don't stay mad at each other anymore.

Take last night for instance, when I stumbled
in drunk in the middle of the night
and peed all over the toilet seat,

and then you got up for a sleepy wee-wee yourself
and of course arose from the seat soaking wet

and I was furious because you were ostentatiously
toweling off your behind

when you should have been listening to my recitation
of the evening's bar-room combats,

so I said, "Fuck you and your pretty charades,"
and I went to sleep.

Six years ago you wouldn't have spoken to me for weeks,
but tonight when I came home
you had dismissed it all for what it was,
a comically intoxicated episode.

I'm afraid we've been together much too long.

Bill

He was a teacher in the drama department,
an assiduous bodybuilder,
and a rather obvious homosexual.
What primarily distinguished him, however,
was his cock.

Here is how it came to my attention:
a friend and I used to work out
a couple times a week at the faculty health club,
and Bill would usually be in there
busting his ass to add to the already heightened
                                     definition
of his pecs and treps.
He was a genuinely nice guy
and we would always have some compliment for him,
as we sat huffing and puffing
from the strain of the previous set,
on the breakneck pace he set himself.

One afternoon, though, my friend came out of the showers
and said to me, "Did you see *that?*"
"See what?" I said.
"Bill's cock!"
"For Christ's sake, I don't stare at guys' cocks—
what do you take me for?"
"Gerry, pretend you're looking for your shampoo
and go back in and look at it."
"You're crazy," I said, and I continued to resist,
but he continued to insist,
until finally I decided that the simplest thing
would be to conform with his ridiculous demand.

It was the eighth wonder of the world, a meathook,
a king cobra, an inverted replica of George Foreman's
                                     forearm.
What havoc the guy must have wreaked upon his lovers.

We still speak of it,
that banyan root, that howitzer, that missile silo,
that bludgeon, John Henry's hammer,
the creature from the black lagoon.

We speak of it loudly but reverentially
on drunken evenings in crowded silken cocktail lounges,

and, within minutes,
we find we have the place to ourselves.

Have they left us from embarrassment,
or are they racing down the freeway,
hellbent for Long Beach?

a guide to the cinema

chuck and i are sitting in the office
discussing movies
and ray wanders in
and chuck says, "you know that movie
that you told me i really ought to see"
and ray says, "sure, *the last wave.*"
and chuck says, "well, i drove all the way
to huntington beach on a weeknight
on your recommendation
and i'm afraid i didn't come away from it
with the same high opinion you expressed.
in fact, i thought it was pretty bad."

and, turning to the door, ray says,
"i didn't think you'd like it."

requiem for three bar guys

ernest hemingway used to say, "there are people
dying this year who never died before,"

and, in *how it was,* mary hemingway says it became
an all-too-frequent refrain.

well, i walked into the bar yesterday
and there was a schooner on the counter
with some bills and coins in it
and a note attached that read, "flowers for claudio."
"what happed to claudio?" i asked,
and the bartender said, "friday night there was
a disturbance outside his bar and he went out back
and found this guy trying to drag some broad into a car.
claudio intervened, and the woman ran away,
and there was a scuffle, and the guy pulled out a knife
and got claudio in a major artery."

"he died?"
"sure."
"they get the guy who did it?"
"do they ever?"

"i didn't know him."
"he was a good guy, just a young guy
who'd worked hard and saved some money
and got some backing and was trying to make a go
of a place of his own. everyone liked him."

just then a guy down the bar said,
"you knew about nels, didn't you?"
"nels?"
"the engineering professor who always drank
in the 'niner."
"sure, i used to have a beer with him
nearly every afternoon."

New York Punks and California Studs

I haven't even seen a gang in this town,
let alone an individual,
that I'd be afraid of
unless he or they were armed to the teeth,

whereas I doubt there's a guy left in Long Beach
beneath the age of thirty
that I could take.

Two for the Seesaw and One for the Road

If I'm over visiting my kids and want
something from the liquor store,
it's about fifty-fifty whether I'll go get it myself
or whether I'll ask my wife to run over for me,
except that as the evening gets later
and I get more mellow and settled in
the odds improve to about 10-1 that I'll send my wife.

This outrages many of her women friends
and I've even seen a trace of concern
flicker about the eyes of a couple of my own friends,

but all it comes down to
is that she's willing to do this little thing for me
just as I am willing to do many little things for her
and just as, I'm pretty sure, if the chips were down
we'd be willing to do big things for each other also.

Now if, as I have seen happening,
her more militant friends succeed in convincing her
that there is something demeaning in her
running these errands for me,

will this truly be a "liberation,"
the "raising of a consciousness"

or just another sacrifice of the amenities to orthodoxy.

Illumination

Unlike everyone else in America,
I have never gotten laid at the laundromat.

Then again, it's my girl who does the laundry.

I'm going to have to end this poem right now—
something just occurred to me.

Divorcee

all the poets complain of her.
they say her child is always crying
in the bedroom while they're
trying to get comfortable on

the couch. i have not found
this true. her child would like attention,
but he'll go where he is told.
her living room is neat and tasteful.

if she's a trifle too solicitous
to make you feel at home,
such thoughtfulness is easily forgiven.
her life is not an easy one.

although she has her guilt, fears, loneliness,
she is scrupulous their mention to avoid.
she has whatever type of music suits your taste;
you know she really can't afford so many records.

her liquor cabinet does not run dry,
but she appreciates it if you bring your own.
she reads more quickly than you do
and can converse on many topics.

in bed she is experienced and giving.
she would like to stay,
but she knows you won't.
she does not expect love.

i like the way she's made ends meet
and some day someone she deserves will stay.
the poets have been so busy looking for poems
that as usual they've missed the point.

at 37

i realized for the first time today
that i'm too old to be drafted now.
whattaya bet that our next war
will be a good war
and that it will arrive
just when i need a good excuse
to get out of the house.

Love Story

my uncle jack met this pretty girl.
he was in his thirties, she twenty-five,
and they both worked for kodak.
he was divorced, catholic,

so they couldn't marry.
it was the depression then as now.
they went to church together
and, when funds allowed,

they went to florida together.
he lived at home with his sisters,
shoveled the snow for them,
worked on their cars,

and on weekends he went to his friend's.
he always slept at home, perhaps
not to give me scandal, or, for all i know,
perhaps they never slept together.

on weeknights he would eat supper with us,
quietly demolish the republicans,
and then retire to his room
to listen to the radio.

last year, both now retired,
they decided they would move to florida.
he stuck around this winter though
to watch out for my aunts

who can't seem to unload
the old three-story house
their father, fresh from the farm,
built by himself, by hand.

last week my uncle's girlfriend died.
she had a stroke; he found her on the floor.
she was in a coma for a week,
then mercifully died.

they'd been together forty years.
he doesn't know what to do with himself.
he repeats his chores.
he can't sleep.

i'm sitting here in tears
but grief has been dishonored by the juvenile,
the sentimental, the commercial.
otherwise the following clichés might mean something:

that they lived within each other and their
life was better than the lives about them,
that death played a filthy trick on them.
his life is empty now.

Wynken, Blynken

I've been having a little trouble with my eyes of late;
the most obvious symptom is that I blink a lot.

What I've found, however, is that people think
I'm winking at them.
And, invariably, they wink back.
They seem to conclude that I have put my finger
on that rare hidden quality of theirs
that sets them above all other people in the room.
They respect my perspicacity, my unparalleled taste.
We sit out the whole party
signaling across the room our brother or sisterhood
in the secret order of winkmanship.

If I had known about this little gimmick in my youth,
I'll bet it would have taken me a lot farther socially

than did my crushing handshake and my piercing
wolf-whistle.

I Wish They All Could Be California Girls

I think I finally understand what the Beach
    Boys meant:

It isn't so much that California girls are
    tanned, athletic, bright, good natured,
    and simply fun to be with...

and it isn't so much that they come of age early,
    age attractively, and love to party
    till the day they die...

it isn't that a migration of lovelies from around
    the world has supplemented the native
    pulchritude...

it isn't even that they fuck...

it's that they give good head.

The Death of Jean-Paul Sartre

of all people, he must have been
the least surprised by death.
i wasn't surprised by his death either,
not that i knew anything about his health,
but because i must, as part of my job,
have about fifteen minutes communicable knowledge
of current intellectual trends,
and so i am aware that existentialism
is a word only uttered today
by norman mailer, me, and a few retarded philosophy majors,
and i doubt either mr. mailer or the philosophy majors
are complimented by my inclusion of myself.

in college and graduate school, you see,
i basically got by with one term paper.
it was entitled: "the existentialism of..."
you fill in the blank.
"the existentialism of sartre or camus or tennyson or
byron or kit smart or milton (yes, milton) or
chaucer (his retraction posed a problem), or beowulf
or caedmon or the venerable fucking bede."

i wasn't trying to put anybody on—
i'd read every word of sartre and his
commentators and his imitators,
and a lot of professors hadn't,
and I sincerely believed that all great writers
must have been existentialists because,
like all true believers or true non-believers,
i was convinced that for a writer
not to have been an existentialist
would have disqualified him as great.
all of this no doubt was in reaction
to the catholic schools i had attended
where it was taught that all great writers

were, at the very least, latent or closet catholics.
my standard term paper
received about five hundred a-plusses,
while more knowledgeable and ingenious students
received incompletes for their herculean-himalayan
and perpetually unfinished papers on "iconography
in arnold as reflected in victorian furniture."

not only did i preach existentialism,
but i began to live
what i knew to be a distorted, popularized
edition of it.
i'm sure my series of marriages
(perhaps mailer's as well)
owe at least a little to sartre,
although they are neither that simply
explained nor regretted.
and some of my existentialism was,
and i hope still is,
the genuine article.
i lecture once a semester to every class
on sartre's "existentialism is a humanism."
i'd give you the lecture right now,
but, with declining enrollments,
i'd better hope you'll sign up and pay your tuition.

so sartre is dead now,
along with his vocabulary-world,
and moral certainties of religion
are alive again and inhabiting the uncrowded humanities
                                                building
(along with the structure, necessity, and remedial comp.),
there is also talk, of course, of faculty salaries,
student evaluations, and the inevitability of layoffs.
i am among the loudest of the talkers,

because if i were ever laid-off
i wouldn't be able to afford
to mope around the *deux magots*—
i doubt i could even afford the polly magoo anymore—
and moping is becoming a lost art anyhow.

jean-paul, they have cremated your feet,
at which i only metaphorically sat.
strangely enough, however,
my current metaphysical problem remains
whether i am capable of the freedom, the alienation,
responsibility, and angst,

of the either/or

of a marriage/dissolution.

On Violence: A Note to Reviewers

neither rhythms nor images nor anything else on the
    printed page is violent.

it is violent to have your teeth kicked out, and a
    gang rape is violent, and what the freeway killer
    has been doing is violent. literature may be the
    occasion of violence, but violent people do not
    sit down and write about their violence, they go
    out and be violent, so let's quit kidding ourselves
    that our turns of phrase, our oxymoronic sublimations
    are true violence.

in doing so, we do a disservice to the violent and to
    their victims.

Patriotic Poem

alexander haig says there are things
americans must be willing to die for.

he is not talking to me:
he is talking to my children.

my children, let me only call to your attention
that no one asking you to sacrifice your lives
has sacrificed his.

the best year of her life

When my two-year-old daughter
sees someone come through the door
whom she loves, and hasn't seen for a while,
and has been anticipating
she literally shrieks with joy.

I have to go into the other room
so that no one will notice the tears in my eyes.

Later, after my daughter has gone to bed,
I say to my wife,

"She will never be this happy again,"
and my wife gets angry and snaps,
"Don't you dare communicate your negativism to her!"
And, of course, I won't, if I can possibly help it,
and, of course, I fully expect her
to have much joy in her life,
and, of course, I hope to be able
to contribute to that joy—
I hope, in other words, that she'll always
be happy to see me come through the door—

but why kid ourselves—she, like every child,
has a life of great suffering ahead of her,
and while joy will not go out of her life,
she will one of these days cease to actually,
literally, jump and shriek for joy.

shit

this poem is entitled "shit."
it is entitled that
because ray zepeda and i decided
that a novel or, in lieu of that,
a poem, should be entitled "shit."
then, whenever someone said,
"i haven't read shit lately,"
he would be referring to our poem.

the only thing we can't understand
is why andy warhol didn't get to the title
ahead of us.

Character Witness

i took my two visiting daughters,
at that time 15 and 17,
to bukowski's 60th birthday party.

he was a perfect gentleman towards them.

when i went to the head
and they went to get a beer
he even asked them if they had
their father's permission to drink beer.
(they did, but they probably would have,
even if they didn't.)

later, as everyone got drunk,
and after hours of everyone
hanging on his every belch,
bukowski was not a perfect gentleman
to everyone.

but he remained a perfect gentleman
to my daughters.
and i later learned
that while i'd been in the other room
he'd made what must have been a special effort
to say nice things about their father to them.

I Do Belong to the American Federation of Labor!

i'm sitting in the tavern
with some of my fellow sports fans,
all of whom are laborers,
and someone complains that there's nothing
to bet on in the spring
(except for suckering an occasional greenhorn
into a wager on the superstars competition)

and i say, without thinking, "at least it's a good
    time
to get a little work done,"

and Old Jim snorts, "work! you've never done
an honest day's work, Locklin, in your goddamn life!"

which isn't the literal truth,
but, as the guffaws chorus and swell,
i decide this is neither the time nor place
to discourse upon
the spiritual travails of the artist.

Mindlessness Over Matter

in the campus parking lot
i see a bumper sticker that i haven't seen before:
"biology is not destiny."

my first thought is of all those species
for whom biology probably and cruelly
is or was destiny:
the dodo-bird, for instance,
and the snail darter.
and i wonder if man is all that different.

but i'm not ready to swallow socio-biology whole
     either.
and it occurs to me, reflecting on something i read
in *time* magazine, that perhaps we could arrive at
a sort of consensus, compromise bumper sticker,
something like, "biology is only sixty percent
of destiny."

then i get to thinking about what bumper stickers
really signify: the belief that loud, visible,
and repeated statements can transform
or create reality.
i'm teaching a course in short story/short film
(actually i'm taking the course as i teach it)
and i can see that the person who owns the car
that sports the biology/destiny sticker
stands firmly alongside munsterberg and arnheim
and the other formative theorists
in her opposition to kracauer and bazin
and the realists.
she feels that if enough people read her bumper
     sticker
then, even if biology used to be destiny,
it soon will cease to be.

and maybe she's right, i muse,
and maybe i should take a lesson
from her transformational project.

maybe i should trade my car in on
one with the largest bumper in the world
and start plastering it with such hopeful pro-
  nouncements as:

anything ernest hemingway could do,
gerald locklin can do better!

and, gerald locklin is a credit
to the human race!

if i really want to test the power of words,
i should try, *gerald locklin has made*
his mother very proud of him!

for starters, however,
it's probably best i try something
a trifle less arrogant,

something like,
please buy gerald locklin's books.

It Takes, It Takes a Busy Man

he hadn't made a dent
in his list for weeks.
one of the items was "call z."
then one day z's wife called to say
that z had died.

he was ashamed to catch himself
indulging in a feeling of accomplishment
as he crossed "call z" off his list.

The Age of Antibiotics

when i was growing up in the forties
there weren't any immunizations yet
for measles and whooping cough and mumps
and chicken pox, not even for polio.
i didn't get polio, but i got most of the rest.
what made me think of this
is that my kids are home with chicken pox right now,
but they've had shots for all the others,
and they'll probably be back in school in a week.

i was always better in a week too,
but my aunts always prevailed upon my mother
to make me stay home an extra week recuperating
while they took turns taking care of me.
that second week was a bore.
i was an active kid who loved,
if not the confinement of school,
then at least the social and competitive aspects of it.
i suspect the ennui of those second weeks in bed—
the awful daytime radio, the awful reader's digests—
turned me into an early masturbator
and confirmed me as a writer.
i was playing with myself to make the time pass
before there was very much to even get a hold of.

but reading a student's essay the other day
on how she contracted scarlet and rheumatic fever
because a doctor sent her home too soon
from a tonsillectomy,

i remember that five of my aunts' brothers and sisters
had died in a single epidemic week
decades before i was born.

and i realized why i,
the only child of them all,

was kept home that second week.

Shoes to Fill, or Don't Make Me Laugh

i saw today, in *coda: the poets' and writers' newsletter,*
a highly amusing item:

the state university of new york at binghamton
is advertising to fill the chair
formerly held by john gardner.

among the qualifications is that the candidate
possess "similar achievements" to gardner's.

maybe they haven't heard in binghamton
that hemingway, faulkner and edmund wilson
are all also dead.

The Walden/Woodstock Apartments

thoreau was right about the
majority of mankind leading lives
of quiet desperation.

the problem with my neighbors
is that they are not even
quiet about it.

RIVERRUN PAST DICK AND JANE

There are those who consider Finnegans Wake obscure,
but they have not taught Freshman Composition.

Homage to John Cage

No Rush

"my husband works nights," she says.
that throws new light on the subject.
night light.
"your husband ever arrive home unexpected?" i ask.
"only once," she says;
"bad case of stomach cramps."

i met her husband once.
it wasn't my idea.
he's twenty years younger than i am
and played semi-pro football for a steel mill.
he seems like a nice guy, but i suppose that
he's capable, like most of us,
of losing his composure under stress.

"maybe," i tell her, "we should wait
until after flu season."

an uncool yul

a lot of people seem to think
that it's just wonderful how yul brenner,
while he was dying of cancer,
made an anti-smoking commercial
that is playing now,
a year after his death.

they say it's the most effective
anti-smoking commercial ever made.

my first reaction is: what an ignominious
and mechanical form of immortality.

my second is: how old was he anyway? what's
so great about old age? i can testify that
middle age ain't no 24-hour orgasm.

my third thought is that he could at least
have provided a companion commercial
extolling all the joys and pleasures and
triumphs of his life that he associated with tobacco.

if you think i'm a smoker,
you're wrong.
i haven't smoked in twenty years
and i only smoked for a couple of years
when i did. i gave up smoking so that
i wouldn't die thirty years younger
than yul brenner.

but during the time that i smoked,
i really smoked up a storm. i just about out-smoked smokin' joe frazier.
i'd come-a-smokin' out of bed each mornin', smoke
a blue streak through my waking hours, and
smoke myself into submission each evening.

if i were to find out today that i were going
to die in a year i suspect that one of the first
things i might do is take up smoking again.
and i really do wonder what, a few years from
now, will be left to us to make each day
worth looking forward to.

the freedom fighters

her mother ranks cleanliness
just a little higher than godliness,

so when my daughter realizes i've caught her
wiping her hands on her jammies in the kitchen,

she winks conspiratorially,

and i wink back.

a constituency of dunces

"you know," lara says,
"adrienne rich can always count on
five hundred feminists showing up
for her readings.

and amiri baraka and ishmael reed
can count on the blacks.

and politically involved readers
will flock to hear carolyn forché,

and bob and dennis draw the gays.

and gary soto the chicanos.

and ferlinghetti and levertov
have fame and politics both:

i mean, it's not that these writers can't write—
i just mean that they also have their followings
that they can count on."

"where's mine?" i ask.

"your problem," she says, "is that the people
to whom your work might appeal
do not read poetry.
in fact, most of those
who might share your attitudes or viewpoint

either don't or can't read at all."

minimal affirmation

i'm reading in a british book on contemporary
literature a chapter entitled "minimal affirmation,"
which tries to microscopically locate the barely
visible ways in which we

bored betrayed despairing disenchanted
defrocked alienated fragmented impotent
uprooted nihilistic dissipated dissociated
defeatist defeated and indisputably MINOR

writers of the generations since WWII

have conspired to burp forth a barely audible
yea,
and i have to run off to give
a poetry reading,
and afterwards, of course, we all congregate
at the reno room to get drunk,

and someone asks me what it was like
teaching college in the 1960s
and without a second thought
i blurt out the eminently un-ennui-like,
"it. . .was. . .

JUST FUCKING GREAT!!!"

On the Rack

i know she is hypersensitive
about her athletic stature,
her pretty smile,
her general wholesomeness,
which everyone except her considers attractive.

so i never miss a chance to allude to
farmers' daughters, sturdiness,
good breeders, and germanic stock;

and since i know she is insanely jealous,
i seldom let an evening go by
without a mention of some beautiful
and temporarily available woman
that i've run into earlier in the day;

and because she's needlessly self-conscious
about her weight,
i wouldn't think of letting a day go by
without suggesting that i run out for
a matterhorn pizza
lest she collapse within the hour
of malnutrition.

if she were a puritan,
i'd ridicule her for that,
but since she loves sex
and has few inhibitions,
i do my best to make her feel
like a nymphomaniac.

these are the ways in which i keep her
anxious, humble, and dependent.
these are the ways
in which i punish her.

and what was her offense:

that she restored my confidence
when i was nearly broken
on the rack.

83

found poem

"Well," Larry says,
"I handed in my found poem."

"Yeah?" I say,
"Where did you find it?"

"Poetry of Chicago," he says.

my mother's funeral

i hadn't slept well, but i had at
least stopped drinking and gone to bed
a couple of hours earlier than usual.
so i wasn't really hungover. my aunt offered
me a shot in my recuperative ginger ale,
but i turned it down: "it's a little
early in the day even by my standards,"
i said, which was true for my regimen in
california, while in rochester, of
course, there'd been little to do *except*
drink.

the funeral was scheduled for 11:00 a.m.
we were in the midst of the July upstate
humidity and i had surprised my aunts by
donning my only sport coat purchased for
my son's wedding, and a borrowed tie. nothing
matched, but one of my aunts is blind and
neither stands on formality nowadays.
i couldn't figure out how to increase
the air conditioning in the limo and the
young driver offered no assistance.

but there was a slight breeze in the
bright contemporary church. this was to
be my first experience of the New Mass
(not to be confused with the New Masses)
and it was destined not to be felicitous.
why, for instance, had i, who had risen
to Second Master of the Altar Boys, ever
bothered to learn all that latin in the
first place? thunderous, resonant, pliant,
plaintive, *Sacred. Mysterious.* loaded with
the *Centuries,* with the *Inexplicable,*
the *Ineffable,* the *Transcendent.*
except for a couple of borrowings from

85

the good ol'anglican hymnal, the new
English version lacked even the power of
a true vernacular, a genuine populism.
Thou Has Conquered Pale Sociologist!
the words and "sentiments" alike tinkled
cheerily along like the bromides of a best-selling
self-help book. we were all returned to pre-school,
the parkinsonian priest not excepted. he, sent
down from canada to die, took a quick dislike to
me as i disdained to sing along or to intone
the jejune responses. i did sort of join in
on the occasional oldie-but-goodie like the
lord's prayer. they hadn't been able to fuck that
one up too bad, no more than some garage band can
really vitiate "shoo-doop-'n-shoo-be-doo," or sid
vicious travesty "my way," or jimi hendrix's the
national anthem. but here's one that i'm sure will
shock you just as much as it did me: they had a
WOMAN running around up there! A FEMALE! A
middle-aged wife and mother who obviously should
have known better. they even let her read from
the goddam pulpit. frankly, i think she was
secretly *running* the whole show, which is exactly
what they should have expected when they gave her
the first inch. i swear, i just about had to be
revived with smelling salts.

and listen to this: the priest came down
and personally offered me communion. i
mean, i'm sure the guy knew i've been doubly
or triply excommunicated on excessively matrimonial
and other grounds, blasphemy no doubt included,
and there he was expecting me to partake of his
little patty-cake rather than spoil the tea-party.
i waved him off like a recovering alcoholic
at a wine-tasting. so did my daughters. but

my son, who's only been inside of a church
about twice in his life (and one of those was
the methodist joint he was married)—
well, my son is a great guy who would hate to
hurt anybody's feelings so he just popped
that wafer like your ordinary m-and-m, while
i cringed in expectation of the lightning.
then, the more i thought about it, well, i
always did have a hard time keeping a straight
face in church, even when i believed it literally,
every word of it—vince prestianni and i were
always managing to get each other snorting,
our shoulders shaking, as we were supposed to be
assisting the priest to load the incense into
the censor at benediction. and now i had a great
deal of trouble not just letting rip with cascades
of glee at the whole grandly magnificent joke
that the catholic church had played on itself,
a gutless, aimless, and emasculated woodstock
without the soul. but my mother wouldn't have
liked that and, after all, even though her being
dead had nothing to do with my mirth at that
moment, it was her big day. and i like my
aunts a lot. and vince prestianni was four
rows behind me where i couldn't set him off.
and i really was impressed by and appreciative
of how many friends of my mother, often lifelong
and in their eighties also, had not merely
bothered but had found the physical capacity
somehow to get to the church. we all talked
too long on the steps, keeping the dour priest
and well paid undertakers waiting. and again
at the grave. most of these mourners, nearly
all of them women, i had not seen in
three decades.

later i wondered if i would ever really
dare to joke about my mother's funeral.
well, folks, i found it actually came
quite easily. and it just came to me
why the priest kept hanging around at
the grave, not talking to anyone, just
clutching his missal to his chest and
glaring upwards—
i'm sure now that i was supposed to
tip him! nobody told me to, and i'm
virtually certain my aunts didn't either,
but i kind of have this vision from my
altar boys days and from my father's funeral
of someone slipping the celebrant a
discreet envelope well line with the
old cashola. no doubt this manly task
should have devolved upon the only surviving son.

ah well, what's one more howler
on a such a hilarious morning.

st. francis would have approved

my aunt Lebou, in her dotage,
used to feed the mice
in the pantry
that the rest of my aunts
were setting traps for.

ancient math

i have always endeavored to improve
the quickness of my children with numbers

by playing a lot of card-games with them,
such as blackjack and gin rummy,

where they had to make calculations on sight.

today, i overheard my youngest daughter
telling a school friend:

"my father taught us how to count:
2,3,4,5,6,7,8,9,10, Jack, Queen, King, Ace."

From a Usually Reliable Source

As our little boy goes running off
to the playground,
my wife says to the headmaster
"He lives in his own world; he has
not yet entered reality."

And the Welsh headmaster
tells her not to worry
that her son is just wonderful and
that someday she will turn around and
discover that he has entered
the world of adult reality.

And she looks the
Welsh headmaster
in the eye
and says,

"Maybe—but his
father never did."

At the University College of North Wales at Bangor

Most of my students here are very poor.

I seldom see them in the pubs: they
cannot really afford the prices.

As winter hits they have to decide whether
to spend their shillings on the coin-operated heaters
or on food.

I suspect that heat often wins—you can
freeze to death quicker than you will starve.

Their incentive is that they will presumably
have more comfortable lives if they survive
the minimalist conditions of college.

The government gives them a small grant
from which to buy books.
We are encouraged to require
very few books.

A book is a valued art object here.

I never hear a complaint here
and no one missed a tutorial
without the most profuse and formal
of apologies.

In California my students and I and everyone else,
also including the movie stars and politicians and
pro-athletes,

seldom stop for breath
in the midst of constant bitching.

You, Gail Sheehy

i'm so sick of hearing the catch-phrase "mid-life crisis"
every time a man leaves his wife
for a younger woman.

when i was twenty-four
i left my twenty-three-year-old wife
for a younger woman.
was that a mid-life crisis?

and when i was thirty
i left my twenty-seven-year-old wife
for a younger woman.
was that a mid-life crisis?

when i was thirty-nine
i fell in love with
the thirty-three-year-old woman
i'd been living with for eleven years.

was that a mid-life crisis?
or a mid-life non-crisis?
or a mid-life anti-crisis?

i'll tell you what it was—
it was a big fat fucking mistake.

el amor brujo

love turns gold to GOLD and
silver to the skin of the agave.
love knows the thirst of the
Mojave lizard and, like the
saint, is never hungry. the
breasts and womb of love
defy all surgeries. the
lovewitch tells man when to
sink the blade and when to
sheathe it. the lovewitch
wakes him from his making
and exhorts him down the
yucca canyons of the double
helix in the several directions
of his love-strewn histories.
love knows all dances, love
invented them, and love knows
that the dance of death is but
one dance of many and death
passeth as it pisseth in
its petty pacing. love needs
no belief in any life but this,
for love has never lost a single
life to death. love clicks its heels.

mannequin

the first naked woman
you can really see
is not your mother
but the mannequin.

you're on the bus downtown.
it is slush and cinders.
they have left her undressed in the window.
the bus stalls, stertorous, for eternity.

all those mounds and slopes
as smooth as aspen, colorado.
you will look for her in aspen,
in the most expensive restaurants.

you will look for her
in paris, tokyo, new york,
wherever fashion reigns.
your dream is to undress her.

we are not talking
of the love of dolls;
we want no sigmund freud
to crack our icon.

ocean, mountain, plains—
more woman than woman;
the brakes of the bus
poison the snow:

we shall not love another.

the woman i'm going out with believes in god

she may be the first woman i've gone out with
in about twenty years
who believes in god.
i mean, she *really* believes in him—
she prays to him, she chats with him,
she isn't nuts, just religious.
she isn't puritan: she smokes and
drinks and we are working on other
aspects hedonistic. she is kind
and responsible and tolerant.

of the jerry falwell types
she says, "i've never understood
why a christian would believe that
god is so small he can't fight
his own battles."

my kinda guy

leaving the downtown bar at closing,
i hear this one young guy say to his buddy,
"you got any beer at your place?"

and the buddy says, "i got some colombian
and a little coke
and there's a guy right in the neighborhood
would bring over some heroin."

and the first guy says,

"yeah, but do you have any beer?"

what i learned from watching the pink panther cartoon festival

never position yourself behind a door,
beneath the matterhorn,
downstream from a dam,
in the middle of an intersection,
or under a truck.

and for god's sake
never never never never never
deposit a bomb in

what you are sure is

someone else's pocket.

my six-month old daughter

my six-month old daughter
must sleep in a strange crib tonight.

who can blame her for crying?

every bed i've ever slept in
has seemed strange.

shadows

these candles never cast a shadow.
suddenly it's more than breath
can manage that the consciousness
can only speak itself,
and that, in spite of aspens, willows,
and the ponderosa where the
breath is thin, it cannot *not* speak.
Fill your lungs with shadows,
young man, speak
of an eternity that curves
like rows of vines
along a darkened hillside:
eclipse the other.

he need regret nothing

when my father was informed
upon the returning in his late thirties
from world war two
that the hundred pounds he'd lost
were the result of diabetes,

he shot himself with insulin every day
and he watched his diet
and he took his urine tests
and he went to work every day
while doing his best
to tread the tightrope between
coma and insulin shock,

and he put up with my mother
and he attended all my athletic events
and every night he sipped imperial blend
with water back.
he said it was only beer and wine
that he wasn't supposed to drink,

but his sister, my aunt bea, once told me,
"i used to say to your father,
ivan, the doctor said you could
drink a *little!*"

still he never got really drunk
nor even really hungover
although i suppose the hiram walker
helped to usher in
some of the episodes when he would have
to be hospitalized.

he died early, aged about fifty, of a heart attack,
just after i finished high school.
he was a very good father to me.

i suppose he could have lived longer
without the evening whiskey
but as it is he died quickly and cleanly—
he died before he could lose
his eyesight, his arms, his legs,
or his son.

Old Nassau's Black Sheep

i'm experiencing some typical fatherly concern
because my daughter blake,
having survived my poem, "poop,"
is going off to teach english for a year
in macao, cinematic capital of opium dens,

and my buddy ray attempts to reassure
me with "graduates of princeton,
gerry, have a tendency not to do too
badly for themselves in life,"

and i sip my vodka-and-tonic and think,

you know, he may be right; the only
downright fuck-up i can think of off-hand
who ever came out of princeton was
f. scott fitzgerald.

my daughter and the firebird

the firebird broods like yeasty dough
upon the embers of his other life.

the firebird designs himself a constellation
of the luckiest houses,
the thirteenth.

the firebird has many eyes
as he wants to have
or none at all.

the song of the firebird
is a polychromatic and synchronic
flame.

when my daughter dances
her heart is in a chord
with that of the firebird.

when my daughter sleeps
her head rests in the feathers
of the firebird aflame
upon a golden bough.

the firebird will shine forth
like a shook papyrus.

he will make an arctic expedition
in the wink of one cold eye.

he will take the form of the denuded
hill of autumn.

he will take the form
of the fire in brandy.
he will captain the sunken galleon.
he is dancing along the christmas log.

soon enough, the christmas log
will expire, but the firebird shall not.

soon enough, no doubt, so shall i,
but our love will live on in the firebird.

I've Always Enjoyed Her Sense of Humor

She's an old friend
and I don't see her very often,
but she has a way of turning up
when I'm talking to a girl I've just met,

and she will invariably storm up to us
and confront me with, "where is the child support check?!"

Then turn her heel and storm from the room,
leaving me to make inadequate explanations.

Why I Go to Art Exhibits

it isn't because of the originals are always
superior to their reproductions: some
are; some aren't. sometimes the galleries
are inappropriately lighted. almost
always they are overcrowded, and the
stage whispers are ludicrous. usually
one searches in vain for a place
to rest one's ass.

it isn't just because, afterwards, we
treat ourselves to meatloaf, borscht,
stuffed cabbage rolls, pierogi at
gorky's café by the deserted flower markets.

it isn't even that i drive us home
on surface roads through neighborhoods
we otherwise would have no knowledge of.

it isn't even that i cherish these
rare days alone with my daughter,
my son, my wife.

it's that for a few suspended moments i
am inches away from a piece of cloth
that has somehow, through the mysteries
of commerce, compromise, and coincidence

made its way to me from the human being
who worked with it. it is a relic and
talisman, more authentic than
the shroud of turin.

Open Admissions

i was talking to charles webb
about the old standby rejection slip,

"we're sorry to inform you that
your manuscript does not fit our
editorial needs at this time,"

and it occurred to me how many women
have issued me pretty much the same
peremptory dismissal—i didn't fit
their current needs—

whereas when i think of all the women
i didn't turn away
even though they didn't precisely fit
into my present needs and plans,

well, i can actually feel something
beginning to glow, a sort of halo.

The New Kids on the Quad

The great critics of modern literature,
such as Edmund Wilson, Richard Ellman,
and William York Tindall,

took extremely difficult works
and made them accessible.

These post-modernist critics
take much less difficult works
and render them incomprehensible.

on the death of a great comedian, spring 1994

i knew he had just gotten over a
two-year bout with tuberculosis,
but the first time i heard that he was
ill again was when he replied to a
student of mine working on an m.a. thesis:

"sorry. can't help you. i have
leukemia."

the next i heard
from rob cohen of *caffeine*,
was that he was out of the hospital
and responding well to the chemotherapy.
later i was to hear,
from his longtime publisher, john martin,
that he'd gone back in
but only to have a few remaining
"bad cells" zapped,
and from marvin malone that,
after a hiatus,
he had begun receiving submissions from him
again for *the wormwood review*.

so just about a year ago
i sent him a letter
absolving him from his usual prompt response,
but telling him in effect
(i don't keep carbons),
"you've won the war.
you've accomplished what you set out to.
i *hope* you're going to stick around
with us for many years yet,
but i *know* your writings will.
from here on in (to paraphrase raymond carver)
it's *gravy*."

110

and last fall,
lying in an intensive care ward myself,
hooked to oxygen and i.v.'s and every
monitor in the hemisphere,
bleeding from the anti-coagulants
and awaiting surgery,
it occurred to me that i might
precede him to the pearly gates
(or the other ones)
and i laughed because,
for a writer,
except as concerns his children and
a very few others,
the sticking-around-in-the-flesh part
is really a distant second,

and i laughed a second time,
glad to have left instructions in my will
against the burial of my remains
in case he should be tempted to fulfill
his oft-repeated pledge
to piss on all our graves,

and i laughed a third time
just because
it seems to me
the only response
(except for the tears at leaving those
one loves)

that death deserves.

The New Male

i just read in *usa today* that,
according to a study published in *lancet,*

"the amount of sperm produced by the
average man has dropped by half
in the last fifty years."

hypotheses include environmental
pollution and snug undergarments;

private investigator locklin suspects
feminist intimidation.

Political Poems

why not just write
a letter-to-the-editor?

yeah, i know it's not as sexy
as being "a committed poet,"

but you'll be published while
the issue is still an issue;

you'll reach a great many more
readers; and you won't

be preaching to the converted.

The Last Round-Up

once in a while i wish there were a god,
mainly so that he could preside,
as vengefully as possible,
over a real lollapalooza of a last judgment.

it's not that i consider my soul to be stainless.
hardly.
i'm quite aware of the commandments i have broken,
and the people, often loved ones,
i have hurt.
if there does prove to be a deity,
i indeed expect that i'll be serving some hard time
for a good long sentence
if not (worst case scenario)
for eternity.

but it would be worth it just to see
the smug ones get their come-uppance,
not just the big criminals,
the serial killers, and the savings-and-loans crooks,
and the harry limes,

but all the petty bullshitters,
the shuck-n-jivers,
the slip-n-sliders,

all those who seem able to go through life
not only lying to everyone else
but even kidding themselves,
never experiencing the slightest self-doubt
or pang or remorse.
i really would love to see those fuckers
and fuckeresses
as they wake up from their complacent sleeps
to find themselves being stared down by
a tribunal of righteousness and wrath.

i'd also get a kick out of witnessing
the looks on the faces of those
who have presumed to put HIM in a dress.

you know, i never realized jonathan edwards and i
had so much in common.

I Am Not Gerald Locklin

i have always hated the name "gerald."
i used "gerald" when i was first writing
because i thought a writer was supposed
to use a formal name. i even, as only
marvin malone and a handful of others
remember, sometimes stooped to "gerald
ivan locklin" to lend a spurious poeticism
to my fledgling literary productions. today
i still use "gerald i. locklin" on official
documents because there are obviously so many
"gerald locklins" running all over the place.

i was named after an uncle gerald who
died young, before i was born, of
tuberculosis. he was supposedly a
very nice man, but, even aside from
the consumption, i never wanted to be him.
as a child i didn't even want to be "gerry":
i was given that name in school. at home
i was "jodie," a name i personally garbled
for myself in the crib. presumably i did
not also give myself the female spelling
of the name, but that never bothered me.

today only two people still call me "jodie":
my only surviving aunt and ron koertge.
sometimes ron calls me "bear," which was
given me by my first and only good karate
teacher twenty-five years ago, just before
he got busted in a hot car. "bear" is
flattering, so of course i don't mind it.
sometimes my wife also calls me "jodie,"
but there is mockery in her voice. i call
myself "toad" sometimes, especially in
poems, although that toad is not always
myself. john owen also calls me that,

116

loudly when i run into him in public.
george carroll does too. and paul the
bartender. they call me that affectionately,
i think.

i guess my favorite nowadays is simply "ger."
when people call me that they seem to be
really getting a kick out of it. i have always
enjoyed being a source of amusement for people.
frankly, i often find myself rather amusing.
and "ger" sounds youthful, boyish, as i frequently
wish i still were. yes, just call me "ger," and i
promise to spare you all tales of white whales.

Sartre Misunderstood

i frequently hear people saying,
"in the words of jean-paul sartre,
'hell is other people.'"
actually sartre never said that:
a character in his play *no exit* did.
and the three characters trapped together
in that little room are all in what sartre
would have called *mauvaise foi,* or
"bad faith." they are, in other words,
trying to deny their freedom, their
responsibility, and to blame their lives
on other people. they don't want to admit
that hell is a state of their own making,
and that while their self-deception
may make them hellish for others to deal with
as well, it all starts in the inferno
of their own self-absorption.

marlow's faust learned this;
so did goethe's.
so, of course, did sartre.

Good Neighbor Pete

twice a week my neighbor saves
all of us on the street from sweeper tickets.
when i hear my doorbell ring
at noon on a thursday
i know i've forgotten to move my car
to the other side of the street.
when it rings on friday i know
i've forgotten to move it back.
i rush out in my stocking feet
to save myself the fine.
up and down the street
others are doing the same.
i tell pete i'd sooner put a match
to a twenty dollar bill
than contribute another cent to this city.
and nowadays the meter maids of both sexes
will write you up from a distance
as long as they can read your license plate
even if you're in the act
of moving your car,
and naturally the one thing the state
is doing better is making
the license plates more visible.

pete is retired but it's not as if
he doesn't have plenty to keep him busy,
including seemingly dozens of kids and grandkids,
not to mention the inevitable jobs around
the house and yard and garage
that he's good at and i'm not.
it's just that he also believes
in being a good neighbor.
if that's a middle-class, republican value,
i hope it spreads to other factions as well.

119

David Hockney: *My Bedroom*

how neat, how english.
how purified of passion.
i realize that it deliberately states
i am not van gogh.

how true.

David Hockney: *De Longpre Avenue,* 1976

five years earlier i met bukowski
in his bungalow on de longpre,
between normandie and western.

hockney's segment,
of palms, pastels, clear skies,
neat dwellings,
must have been
considerably west of there.

To Get What You Pay for Is The Best You Can Expect

i overheard how bukowski had these
incredibly reasonable mortgage payments
on his very nice house in san pedro
and yet he had this constant worry that
he wouldn't always be able to make them.

i can understand that. he didn't, after all,
have a steady job, and who would not be a fool
to count on the continuance of literary income,
especially anyone who'd known the years when
royalties were zilch.

so he knew well the way employers and the government
can get you by the balls, and now he had a chance
to learn, before dying, the way s-and-ls can
get their claws into you.

so why did he do it?
no doubt partly for his wife,
a woman whom he loved and who was giving him
a better life than he had ever known,

but he also enjoyed the place,
the garden and the view,
a good place to raise cats,
a bit of spaciousness, a little privacy,
room to garden, room for a narrow lap-pool.
some shelves to keep his books on,
improved audio for bruckner and ludwig b.,
some neighbors and some distance from them,
a little girl across the street who
brought out the grandfather in him.

and who really wants to end up living in the gutter,
dying in humiliation?
so, a little mortgage-worry wasn't all that bad a
                                        trade off.
and anyone who thinks that you don't pay for
what you get in life
is either an old fool
or a very young one.

Summer School

it is june again and i am teaching
five hours a night, four nights a week,
for five weeks. i kid that i am doing it
for the pure love of teaching, but,

of course, financial considerations have
exerted their influence, a major one.
still, i do not speak entirely with
irony. it is a good time to be

teaching. the days are warm; the
evenings cool; the sun sets late.
there are no faculty meetings,
no battles over personnel or policies.

the spring semester has not yet
ended for my wife and children;
thus, i have the house to myself
during the day. three or four times

a week i swim and lift a few light weights
at the y.m.c.a. i only eat one meal a day,
and so i make it something i enjoy, most
often italian or mexican. the rest of the

time i read and write and teach. it's
a wonderful life. do you know what a pleasure
it is to declaim "the windhover" and "fern hill"
to twenty bright and motivated students?

to communicate my love of *the sun also rises?*
to explain how faulkner's historical determinism
accounts for his stylistic complexity?
to introduce them to bukowski, koertge, field,

and haslam? to chat with them on our breaks
near the diet coke machine about their jobs and
kids, about mine? to join a few of them after
the final exam for the ancient ritual of a few

beers, even if mine these days are of the non-
alcoholic variety? don't get me wrong: i earn
my pay; i work hard for it. i do a good job. i
know my stuff. no false modesty: i'm a good

teacher. but would i do it for free?
yes, if i were independently wealthy.
would i pay for the privilege of teaching?
yes, if i could afford it.

do i look forward to retiring someday?
well, there are aspects of the job that
i could definitely do without, that are
even, no doubt, shortening my life, and

that are certainly a waste of time
remaining in the only life that i will
ever have. but as i said, in summer
one is largely spared of these stresses.

i have been doing this for over thirty
years now. i wish there could be thirty
more…or three hundred. i suppose
that i'll be lucky to last for ten.

maybe only five; maybe fewer. realistically,
i guess i'd strike a devil's bargain
for another twenty. i'd be seventy-four
years old then, in the year 2015.

what inestimable sadness dwells in simple numbers.

The Bunnyfish

it's what i called my daughter
when she was very young
and just learning to swim.
i would pick her up from lessons
at the outer pool,
and every morning she would emerge
with teeth chattering,
she was so slender, so sleek,
her hair wetted back,
and a frown creasing her brow.
i'd sweep her into a long, thick towel,
hug her up into my arms,
and hurry her to the car,
her cold cheek against my warm neck,
rush her home to a hot shower.

now she's a teenager
and these are not easy years
for her or for me.
she thinks i protect her too much,
that her friends have more freedom,
more fun, and maybe they do.
you always hear that you have to
let children learn from their mistakes,
but i don't think you have to let them
make mistakes before they are even
out of high school, out of the house,
that will curtail their lives before
they have even had a chance to live.
so in the necessary tug-of-war of
these years, the tension of her
struggle for independence
(i representing civilization;
she, the discontents of those whose
freedom is restricted) i try at least
to slow things down a little, to let

her have a chance to grow into the
capacity to make the decisions she will
have to make, and i try to assure that
she will have the base of education
that will afford her a life lived
as her own woman.

invariably, though, we are sometimes
hurtful to each other
in our sarcasms and silences.
and if i err in exaggerated fears,
or am sometimes tempted to flee into
the refuge of no longer caring,
from which i am always brought back
by the immensity of how i do care,
i can only hope that she will one day realize
how often she has been
all that i have lived for,
how i gradually turned myself into
a different person,
so i would be a better father to her,
starting back when she was first
her old da's bunnyfish,
shivering in my arms which were still powerful:
i turned my life towards her then,
and now i am simply seeing it through to the end,
an ignorant man in an even more ignorant world,
making mistakes, but making them
out of love for her.

I'm about Ready for the Venerable Bede

when she was a young novelist and philosopher
iris murdoch wrote under the influence
of sartre and wittgenstein.

these days she writes under the influence
of plato.

i suspect that, as one grows a little older,
and the finitude of life becomes palpable,
one returns to those writers who have stood
the test of time, rather than squandering
one's dwindling hoard of hours
on contemporary works of questionable value.

an easy-going weekend

with my wife and daughter away at
my daughter's college for four days,
it has been a bachelor's weekend
for my fifteen-year old son and me.
we get along easily because we
like a number of the
same few basic things: eating,
reading, writing, music. his social
life is different from my current
one: he visits with his friends,
girls and boys, while i swim at
the ymca pool. then he watches
videos—a compromise between
the ones that he picks out—
empire records, strange brew—
and the ones i think he ought to
be exposed to—*citizen kane,
la strada, dr. strangelove.* he
plays his amplified guitar; i switch
a game on when the yankees are
at bat. i give him *in our time*
to read; finish up a flann
o'brien for my class. we both
like italian one day, mexican the
next. he feeds the cats and does
the dishes for his mother.
at night, he works late on
a story at the mac; i write
a poem with a pad and pencil.
i exercise the dog and feed it.
i go to bed before he does.
we both say, "love you; see
you in the morning." and
we mean it.

hot sunday afternoon

my son has kept his sunday afternoon
free to go hear jazz with me.
i swim from noon to two,
lift a few weights,
pick him up at quarter-to-three.
i put on *sketches of spain* on the
tape deck of the taurus as we
head north on the san diego freeway.
he reads his hemingway—mine too.
coming over la cienega, haze and
glare rise from the whiteness basin
but the hills of hollywood still
catch one's breath. miles moves
into solea and my son puts down
his book, broad boulevards almost
deserted, a corner taco stand,
the sidestreet rows of california
bungalows: at times, l.a. is still
the town of philip marlowe,
james m. cain,
nathaniel west if he had not
been a new yorker.

Where Have You Gone, T.S. Eliot?

in the aerobics room,
going nowhere on my treadmill,
while watching a beefy colleague
climb stairs while remaining in place,
it occurs to me that maybe
what we have instead of
st. john of the cross,
the dark night of the soul,
and the subsequent ascent of mount carmel,

is the stepmaster machine.

none too soon

on the art calendar for the met
i notice that "the artist's garden at st. clair"
was a gift, in 1948, of
the harris brisbane dick fund.

with all the philanthropies for
the heart, the lungs, the pancreas,
it's about time someone did a little fundraising
for this modest appendage.

The Nurses

the nurses take their breaks
seriously, and they take a lot
of them. still, they do
have to know how to do an
awful lot of different things,
none of them particularly pleasant
tasks. and most of them are
nice enough if you just show
them a little thanks, say
please, try not to rush
them, and are not demanding.

of course he falls in love
with all the female nurses,
age be damned—this
is probably necessary for
a man, a part of sustaining
his will to recover. and
he searches for signs of
reciprocation, a pat on
the arm, a breast leaned
into his shoulder, an
indication that their
connections are enjoyed.

there will be no catherine
barkley to his lieutenant
henry, of course: he can
barely move and is never
off oxygen. nurses don't
climb into the sack with
patients on the intensive care
and pulmonary floors, in case
you hadn't figured that out.

still, he prefers the female
touch, although the males are
more than capable. he can't
believe how beautiful one guy
with twenty years experience handles
a longshoreman who goes berserk
in the middle of the night,
no panic, just firmness and
quiet understanding of the man's
terror, at the turn his
life has taken. maybe the
nurse has watched his own father
or grandfather have to confront
this same cessation of a
life lived as a man, the
life a man traditionally lived.

no, there will be no romantic
novels written out of this
experience—only a few
testaments of kindness.

Obviously Not a Gambler

the surgeon who is talking me into
allowing him to implant a filter
through my jugular vein and into
the vena cava admits there
is a one or two percent chance that
the little sterling silver device will go
straight to the heart, in which
case, "bingo!"

but he reassures me that he's
already performed the surgery,
without losing a patient,
close to a hundred times.

Toad's Handicap

As a result of lung problems
Toad discovers he has
reduced oxygen capacity.

The most serious consequence
seems to be that it's more difficult
to run away from his responsibilities.

Placing the Blame

an author i have never even met
writes me, "maybe your comforts are
trying to kill you."

that's the new puritanism
with which we live.

people tell me they're doubling their
exercise, even after i've explained
it was my lungs, not heart, and
that i *was* exercising, and that
because the lungs were blocked
with bloodclots, the exercise
was accelerating the damage.

they aren't really listening to
anything i say at all, because
they're sure they already
know the answers, which are
what they've heard on the
evening news: that they can
save their lives through
exercise, diet, abstinence.

and they may in fact
tack a few years on.

"now you start taking care
of yourself," they scold,
convinced that my illness is
a result of my years of
drinking.

and i will take care of myself—
i'll tack on a few years too.

137

but it will only *be*
a few extra years, months, weeks,
for me or for them.

our genes carry our death sentences.

but at least our theories of
clean living relieve us of
having to waste our precious hours
sympathizing with each other.

Running into Ger

lately i've been running into myself

men with salt-and-pepper hair the
length of mine. short ragged beards.
rough facial skin. in jeans and tee shirts.
sometimes heavy as i used to be;
sometimes thin as i've become.

one was at the end of an aisle
at the target discount store
(a cheapskate like myself).
one was an extra on a t.v.program.
one was a biker in the parking lot
of an italian restaurant.

they are never speaking.
they are never laughing.

sometimes they are smoking,
as i did twenty-five years ago.
they always seem to be waiting.

jeffrey weinberg saw a recent photo of me
and said i looked like a survivor of auschwitz.
my alter egos haven't been through
anything that bad.
neither have i.

in many ways i've lived a charmed life.
i wonder if they have.

they all seem to know that
the future cannot be trusted.

The Witnesses Meet My Teenage Daughter

as the interminable bells summon me to
semi-consciousness, i realize my daughter
has already answered the door:

"good morning," they are already chorusing,
"is this a christian household?"

"nope," my daughter says, "we're a bunch of atheists."

wonderful, I silently exult, making a mental
note to reward her with a new compact disc,
and i figure, *now they'll know better than
to pick on a minor—they'll leave their
"literature" and go away and i can roll
back over for another couple of hours.*

but instead i hear them asking her ingratiatingly,
"then you probably don't believe in the biblical
account of God's creation of the universe?"

"nope again," she says, "all of us in this house
believe in evolution, even my little brother."

"oh, and where is *he?*"

"he's on his way to his karate class
in my mother's car."

"well then, maybe you would like to hear
the true story of the creation..."

"that's *enough!*" i bellow,
through resounding tunnels of phlegm,
as i struggle to free myself of the bedclothes.

"what was *that*?!" i hear the witnesses
inquire with a quaver.

"i said *that's enough!*" I bellow,
rolling to my feet.

"that?" my beloved daughter replies,
"oh that was just my father. he's the
BIGGEST atheist of us all."

then i hear the door slam and
her footsteps on the hardwood floors:

"it's okay," she reassures me; "they seem
to be skipping the rest of the homes on this block."

and I suddenly realize that *she* is going to be
okay also.

An Immortal in the Flesh

i come out of my lower-division
poetry writing class with two of
the more talented students

and we are near the hot-dog cart
when i spy an almost young man,
frail and slightly bent, but possessed
of a bright-eyed depth and virility,
making his way across campus
with an armload of spanish books.

"you see that guy?" i say,
"the finest living poet in chile
...make that *latin america*."

the *living* part is significant,
because he as easily could not be,
having been tortured on a torture ship
off the coast of his country
in the days of replacement
of allende by pinochet.

one of them says, "gerry, you're shitting
us again."

so i tell them how raul zurita is here because
my colleague in spanish-portuguese, jack
schmitt, is now his translator for university
of california press, and how raul has just
returned from a reading tour of russia
and the continent and how he will soon
be touring america.

i explain that he speaks little english
and i no spanish
and that he writes oblique poems
and i write short direct ones.

and yet there somehow from the first
has been a warmth of camaraderie between us.

they say, "we just watched a world-class poet
hunch incognito past the hot-dog cart?"

i say "the greatest poet in spanish
since neruda, is what they tell me,

and, from jack's translations,
i believe it."

they're still not sure
that i'm not shitting them.

a nobel prize might assuage
any doubts about raul, but i imagine
they'll still take *my* pronouncements
with a grain of sal hepatica.

Personal Storage

i come upon an ad for "personal storage"
and i think, "yeah, we could all use a
comfortable and private and inexpensive
and purely temporary and voluntary place

to store oneself

(or, as barthes, lacan, and derrida
might put it, *our selves*)

on those occasions when
it or they
become just a bit too much
for us or anyone else
to deal with.

give me a break

in the shopping district of *la habana*
an american woman misplaces a $100 bill
and thinks she either lost it
or inadvertently handed it to a shop clerk
as a bill of much lower denomination.

but she can't just mourn the loss—
i'd be ready to slit my wrist—
no, because she's a liberal
she has to rationalize it:

"wouldn't it be wonderful,"
she repeatedly insists,
"if some poor person got it from me
by mistake—maybe somebody whose children
really needed it for medical expenses—
or who were on the verge of malnutrition—
it would be the equivalent of four months'
salary for a cuban."

and when it turns up,
tucked away very safely and securely,
in a corner of her wallet—
she feels it necessary to add,
"i almost wish i'd lost it;
it would mean so much more
to one of them."

and *i* almost say,

"then why the fuck don't you
just *give* it to someone,

preferably to *me?*"

when the drinking was good

i'm not going to dwell here
on the evils of alcohol
(which are real)
or on all the types of good times
i had when i was drinking either.
this is just about some of the times
when i'd go up to our cabin
at big bear.

if my wife and kids
were already there, i might
stop after the flatland portion
of the ride from long beach to redlands,
usually in heavy traffic,
and pick up a new c.d. or two
at a record store.
then i'd have a beer or two at frank's place,
a roadside bar in mentone "beach,"
where the mainly chicano laborers
were just getting off work.
i'd listen to the talk of bosses,
sports, women, the weekend coming up,
enjoy the vernacular humor,
the poetry of the male idiom,
the hearty, healthy discourse that
twain and whitman tapped into,
that made their work and so much
of american literature that flowed
from them possible. i was comfortable there.

or i might have a couple of vodka-tonics
on the old main street of redlands,
in a dark cocktail bar with a small
pool table and a barmaid who was,
in that lighting, easy to look at
and easy to talk to.

either respite would ease the hour's
drive that i had left up the curving
mountain road.

i'd be glad to pull onto
the gravel driveway of the cabin,
and my kids would be happy
to see me. so i'd have another
for the dust of the highway and we'd
all head out for enchiladas
(beer for me) or pizza (wine for me).
back at the cabin i'd break out my
jug of ernest and julio gallo livingston
cellars cream sherry, in its handsome
blue label that made it look more english
than modesto, while my wife set up the
board for chinese checkers or monopoly.
a little later they'd all head upstairs
to be and i'd sit up till deep into
the night, listening to music,
everything—mahler, rachmaninoff,
satie, barbra streisand, dexter
gordon, keith jarrett—as i wrote
and read and was comforted by
the wild burros rubbing up against
our walls, to scratch their hides,
i guess, and absorb a little of the warmth.
and i often wrote well there,
a *sketches of spain* suite, for one thing,
among the first of my jazz poems—and i read
well too—iris murdoch, *a sportsman's sketches,*
rabbit at rest, the sunlight dialogues.
sometimes i'd close my eyes a while,
but i was not drunk and, believe me, i
would tell you if i had been. i was
intoxicated, though, with the transforming

toxins, ecstatic with the aesthetic.
finally, i'd turn the music off,
close up the writing pad,
put a bookmark in the novel, push the
cork back in the bottle. go up the
stairs to gaze out the picture window
at the dry-lake valley of the erwin
ranches, constellations clear above
the gambrel dwellings, dust or snow
upon the sagebrush, air crisp with
the morning.

i would be the last one up,
of course, and sure i had my share
of headaches, but i'd fix that with
a couple of excedrin, maybe advil,
wash them down with a quart of
rehydrating, recaffeinating pepsi.
a little later i'd be ready for
some toast or english muffins,
maybe even bacon, ready for the flat
sun and the lodgepole pines, the smells
of resin, coffee, charcoal in the air.

it wasn't always that good, naturally.
the same things can go wrong up there
as down the hill, kids having stomach upsets,
disagreements with the wife, along with
other things you only have to deal with
up there, broken water pumps and leaking
pipes, and getting snowed in.

but this is just one for the good times,
the times when alcohol made everything
a little more intense, brightened and
deepened the colors of the day and night,

when it was just what the doctor ordered,
aided and abetted a general sense
of well being and good will.
i loved my children all the more,
felt generously towards my wife,
even experienced some pale beginnings
of romanticism's animistic view of nature.

such were not always the times there—
there were bitter interludes as well—
but i'd be a liar by omission
if i'd didn't testify to these occasions
when the wine-god kept his promises.

i even came to love
(not carnally!)
and now to miss
those ever-humping and absurdly
innocent wild burro families.

Un Bel Di

because my daughter's eighth-grade teachers
are having what is called an "in-service day,"
which means, in fact, an out-of-service-day,

she is spending this Friday home with me,
so i get up in time to take us,
on this summery day in march,
for a light lunch at a legendary café
near the yacht marina.

then we feed some ducks before catching
the cheap early-bird showing of
my cousin vinny, at which we share a
dessert of a box of milk duds large
enough to last us the entire show.

afterwards we drive to a shoe-store to
get her the birkenstocks she's been coveting,

but they're out of her size in green; we leave
an order and stop for dinner at norm calvin's
texas-style hole-in-the-wall barbecue rib factory.

when we get home i am smart enough
to downplay to my wife what a good day
we have had on our own. later, saying
goodnight to my little girl

already much taller than her mother,
i say, "days like today are the favorite
days of my life," and she knows

it is true.

The Iceberg Theory

all the food critics hate iceberg lettuce.
you'd think romaine was descended from
orpheus's laurel wreath,
you'd think raw spinach had all the nutritional
benefits attributed to it by popeye,
not to mention aesthetic subtleties worthy of
verlaine and debussy.
they'll even salivate over chopped red cabbage
just to disparage poor old mr. iceberg lettuce.

I guess the problem is
it's just too common for them.
It doesn't matter that it tastes good,
has a satisfying crunchy texture,
holds its freshness
and has crevices for the dressing,
whereas the darker, leafier varieties
are often bitter, gritty, and flat.
It just isn't different enough and
it's too goddamn american.

of course a critic has to criticize;
a critic has to have something to say
perhaps that's why literary critics
purport to find interesting
so much contemporary poetry
that just bores the shit out of me.

at any rate, I really enjoy a salad
with plenty of chunky iceberg lettuce,
the more the merrier,
drenched in an Italian or roquefort dressing.
and the poems I enjoy are those I don't have
to pretend that I'm enjoying.

151

where we are (for edward field)

i envy those
who live in two places:
new york, say, and london;
wales and spain;
l.a. and paris;
hawaii and switzerland.
there is always the anticipation
of the change, the chance that what is wrong
is the result of where you are. i have
always loved both the freshness of
arriving and the relief of leaving. with
two homes every move would be a homecoming.
i am not even considering the weather, hot
or cold, dry or wet: i am talking about hope.

One to Whom It Is Not a Joking Matter

owner of a base-model hyundai excel,
which, with my affliction of the feet,
knees, back, shoulders, and elbows,
i am often hard-pressed to operate,

i say, "my next car is going to have
automatic transmission, power steering,
power brakes, power windows, maybe even
an ejection seat with a parachute. maybe
i'll even get me one of them rehab vehicles
with a hydraulic lift."

"good," my wife says, "with a car like that
you should be able to drive yourself
to all your doctor's appointments, maybe
even to the hospital."

"in which case," i say, "maybe i won't
have to drive myself home."

"but with a great car like that," she says,
"you'll be able to drive yourself
to the cemetery."

"naturally," I retort, "but by then you will,
of course, have personally chauffeured me
to the poor house and the nut house."

for my wife and me this is just good
wholesome dark humor,
though not without its edge of truth,

but i notice on the face of my daughter,
who loves me and depends on me,
the same first slap of reality
that i experienced when, at her age,

i asked my father how long he thought
he would live. and he said, "oh, according
to the statistics, i'll be lucky if i
last five more years," and the medical odds-makers

had that one figured right on the money.

The Condemned Man's Last Supper

i think i would demand an exact replication
of a seven-course sunday dinner i enjoyed
at vince prestianni's house in 1958,
prepared by his mother, nellie,
presided over by his father, biagio,
and enlivened by his kid brother, benny.

if they turned me down for that feast
(and, to tell the truth,
who could duplicate it?)
i guess i'd settle for
any decent plate of

spaghetti and meat balls,
spaghetti and italian sausage,
or spaghetti and mushrooms.

i don't think, at that juncture
i should concern myself much
about fiber.

rejection slips and slip-ups

this is just the briefest of pep-talks
to any of you young writers who have been
receiving so many rejection slips that
you are on the verge of accepting the
executioner's thumbs-down:

in 1863 a group of artists rejected by
the official parisian salon (i read
on the universe calendar) exhibited at
a salon of their own dubbed
the *salon des refuseés*,
or, "the salon of the rejected."

these included cézanne, monet,
jongkind, guillaumin, whistler,
fantin-lateur, and pissarro.

Where's Wally?

fuck wally.

Jocasta

had a face that
only a mother-
fucker could love.

almond blossom

if you don't look closely at
the rings of the branches,
it could be by anyone.
well, anyone who was among
the greatest painters of the
century: matisse, perhaps.
anyone who had studied
prints from the japanese.
anyone who loved light,
and living things.
anyone who believed in
the rebirth of nature,
the seasons of existence,
the blossoming of the creative.
anyone who had
absorbed the centuries,
had mastered his techniques
and from whose eyes
the scales had fallen.

Van Gogh Died Childless

and it troubled him that his brother, theo, named
a son *vincent.* You can
read about it in *still life,*
a novel by antonia byatt,
a book you should read anyway.

he seemed to find it
a distraction,
a needless extra pressure on him,
an anomaly he did not want
or need.

the sociobiologists see no need
to explain the egotism of the
human: they take it as a given,
the force
that drives us to adapt,
survive, and procreate, to
keep alive "the selfish gene."
it's *altruism* needs explaining.

sometimes it takes the face of
devoting oneself to the children
of others, a sister's perhaps,
as my childless aunt pat
devoted her life to me,
and now i am the one
who has the children
and the grandchildren.

it can be the firemen,
the soldiers, or the
anonymous citizen hero
who lays down his
life to save that
of another.

the mother who dies in childbirth,
the medical researcher,
the schoolmarm,
the priest,
mother theresa,
the pope whom millions of the
poor, the faithful, call out
to as *papa*,
father.

it can also be the artist,
giving all to his art.

van gogh died childless,
but his suns and cypresses and irises
today
make us want to live,
intensely,
and to give life,
share it,
propagate it like
a field of grain.

so young i wrote of him
an unpublished "starry night,"
of course,
about as bad as jim croce's.
i have been more alive
because of him—
we all have.

i am an animal;
we all are;
so was he.

but art lives also,
in a life my dog
in the backyard
does not get to enjoy,
although he loves his food,
and exercise,
and praises,
as much as i do.

i have my son with me today,
he too an artist.

van gogh did not die childless.

Smoking Skulls II

the skull is enjoying its cigarette.
it looks downright happy.

could heaven consist of
untaxed vices

that can't kill you twice?

Roofs in Paris

the rooftops of paris,
the sidewalks of paris,
the cafes and businesses of paris,
the churches of paris,
the three hills of paris,
the windmills of paris,
the boulevards of paris,
the cobblestones of paris,
the parks of paris,
the bridges over the seine,
the cemeteries of paris,
les places of paris,
the theatres of paris,
the prostitutes of paris,
the market-streets of paris,
the schools of paris,
the accordions of paris,
the museums of paris,
the race-tracks of paris,
the hotels, grand and small, of paris,
the thieves of paris,
the quais of paris,
the fishermen of paris,
the fly-boats of paris,
the bookstores of paris,
the fashions of paris,
the breakfasts of paris,
the schoolgirls of paris,
the old ones of paris,
the lovers of paris...

I could go on...

paris exists to be painted
and as
a setting for the unforgettable,

the indelible.
paris exists so that
we may die, know that
we have lived.
paris is everything
that disneyland can never be.
paris does not want
to be some other place.
paris is first.
paris, even with mcdonald's,
is itself.
paris is paris.
paris is not
in nevada.

Deconstruction, Decentering, Demythologizing

new words for
old lies.

No Longer A Teenager

my daughter, who turns twenty tomorrow,
has become truly independent.
she doesn't need her father to help her
deal with the bureaucracies of schools,
hmo's, insurance, the dmv.
she is quite capable of handling
landlords, bosses, and auto repair shops.
also boyfriends and roommates.
and her mother.

frankly it's been a big relief.
the teenage years were often stressful.
sometimes, though, i feel a little useless.
but when she drove down from northern california
to visit us for a couple of days,
she came through the door with the

biggest, warmest hug in the world for me.
and when we all went out for lunch,
she said, affecting a little girl's voice,
"i'm going to sit next to my daddy,"
and she did, and slid over close to me
so i could put my arm around her shoulder
until the food arrived.

i've been keeping busy since she's been gone,
mainly with my teaching and writing,
a little travel connected with both,
but i realized now how long it had been
since i had felt deep emotion.

when she left i said, simply,
"i love you,"
and she replied, quietly,
"i love you too."

you know it isn't always easy for
a twenty-year-old to say that;
it isn't always easy for a father.

literature and opera are full of
characters who die for love:
i stay alive for her.

Happiness

so many people search for it.
this search for personal happiness
becomes all their lives are about.

i was raised to think in terms of
accomplishments, for oneself or
for others, of goals, of striving.

rest was something for the next life;
peace was something to put off till eternity.
happiness was a static thing to want,
an artificial and impossible paradise.
better to keep on trying to accomplish
what one has set out to accomplish
in one's life.

and yet, without seeking it,
and even now that i've quit booze,
or maybe especially now that i've quit
booze,
i often find that, momentarily at least,
i am extremely happy, even quietly ecstatic.

and sure i get "stressed out," especially
when i take on or have thrust upon me,
more than time realistically allows,

but something tells me that,
in spite of struggle, strife, and tension,

and regardless of what the future brings,

i have known, on balance, much
more happiness
than those who go through life thinking
that it's playing hide-and-seek with them.

Was Charles Bukowski a Better Writer than William Shakespeare?

no.

everyone lives a lie

i always insist on
the fictionality of everything i write—
or, in fact, the fictionality
of all our versions of our lives,
even those we *want* accepted as
autobiographical truth, because we simply
do not have direct, transparent access
to the past, or even to the
present which, in the instant it takes
to reflect upon it, has already
turned into the past, into history,
into a story we are re-constructing to
suit our own psychic needs of survival.

and i try to discourage my students
from asking of each other's poems,
"did that really happen?" or
from thinking that it improves their
own to claim it really did.

there are good legal, professional, critical,
and personal reasons to insist on
this fictionalizing as well, as the
sign on the wall of an old
friend, a cop, read:
"admit nothing."
it's a lesson the young will probably
have to learn, like most things,
the hard way.

still, i always assumed that
edward field's long poem of sexual
self-discovery during wwii was
"autobiographical" because he has
historically been self-revealing in his work,
only to learn from him now that

171

it is a version of a movie script
that he and his friend neal devised
but didn't manage to sell.

of course it is in every artistic
way "true," truer than the literal
truth, a mirror in which so many
may see the truth of their own
identities, so true in its fiction
that i could not help but be
compelled to read it as the
truth.

the loser

in the 1980's
the students at universities
where edward field read his poems
regarded him as a loser:

"queer," unfamous, unrich,
and less than a real man.

it was a decade of winners
the decade in which
we trounced the russians,

and field's only talent
was to put into words—
simply, unadorned, yet
musically, rhetorically, and
metaphysically organized language—

the common experience of americans,
of human beings,
especially as expressed in
our popular culture.

such a limited activity.
such a lack of ambition.
and there was even some question
whether he was truly happy.

in the nineties,
the winners died,
and they are still dying today,
as william carlos williams put it:

"miserable for lack of what
is found in poetry."

forget the sexual politics

i witnessed a poet break down
while reading a poem dealing with
his love for the man he lived with
and cared for (his companion being blind)
for maybe thirty years, maybe more.

he tried a number of times to go on,
but finally gave up.
this has almost happened
to me
while reading certain poems
about my love for my daughter.

the moment clarified for me
a simple truth
that I had always known
intellectually, even emotionally,

but had never experienced such
a vivid memorable
demonstration before:

love is love.

amedeo modigliani: reverdy, cendrars, et cetera

why do poets have to affect
such a depressing air
of self-importance?

(probably because they know
how thoroughly expendable
all but a few are.)

amedeo modigliani: *pencil portrait of hans arp*, 1916

he was a professional smart-ass,
but you can tell he had
a good arp.

amedeo modigliani: *seated nude with folded hands,* 1918

his nudes so often
situate their hands upon
their laps, if clothed,
their genitals, if not.

this has an interesting
and paradoxical effect:
of modesty at war with masturbation.

i think the artist knew this,
and i think it turned him on.
i think subliminally and maybe overtly
that the models knew it too.

i think they all knew
i would like it.

men are from mars; women are from bellevue

i read in kurt vonnegut the conclusion:
"men are jerks; women are psychotic."

it may be true.

certainly every woman i've ever
been involved with
has had at least episodes
of acting nuts,
and they've all considered me,
at least at times,
a jerk.

of course women might argue
(in fact they *do*)
that it is our being such jerks
that forces them to act so irrationally.

while i might venture that
another of their traits is
blaming everything on us.

ah well, it must be necessary for
the survival of the species.
probably the genders would be well advised
not to be in too great a rush
to change each other.

the conqueror

lately i'm early-to-bed
and early-to-rise.
so far, early bird that i am,
i still haven't gotten the worm.
but it won't be long
before the worm gets me.

enzo cucchi: *i uno*

push the envelope.
push the envelope.
push the envelope.
until it envelopes us.

put the amiable skulls
to be together.
tuck them in
beneath the sheets
up to their absent necks.

offer yourself up on a platter.
offer yourself up *as* a platter.
offer yourself up as
a blue plate special.

your shapely legs remain.

swim sunlight.

paul klee: *this star teaches bending*

the black of death
upon the blue of dying

born burning, the star
is always burning down.

flaming into being, the
star is always flaming out.

the star, knowing it is
creature, not creator,
created not creation,
teaches us to genuflect.

this star invents the wheel.
this star is struggling to
evolve into a face.

this star is a matrix to
a progeny of stars,
each a nucleus,
each with iron spokes.

this star is a horse.
this star is a hobby horse.
this star is a rocking-horse loser.

the back of the baby horse is convex;
that of the daddy horse, concave.

this star has learned humility;
it teaches us humility.

the strength of the proud: humility.

light bends;
space is curved;
space is carved creatively.

181

the ultimate pessimist

he could never decide
whether his cup
was completely empty,

or whether perhaps
there just wasn't
anything in it.

henry's gift

my swedish friend,
henry denander,
whom i've never met,
sends me a zoot sims cd
from 1984 with the suggestion,
"put it on and forget about
your busy day at the university."

because he doesn't send me
the liner notes or album cover
i can't get all involved in trying to
expand my limited technical and
historical knowledge of this music
that i love so much.
"easy listening but a wonderfully
relaxing album," he adds, and he's right,
i do find time to just sit back and listen,
and i do relax, do nothing else,
let my mind wander as i might under the
massage of a long, hot shower.

our enemies are blowing up our buildings, and
would like to blow our bridges too.
anthrax is in the air.
small pox wants to come back from the dead
and spoil my pretty face.
saddam and bin laden would like
to go ballistic,
every time i turn on cnn,
i get uptight,
but i can't leave it off because
i might be the last guy in town
to learn of an evacuation order.

maybe that would be best anyway.
that's how zoot's strophes make me feel,
as mellow as lingonberry pancakes,
as absolutely laid-back as *absolut,*
as sane as dead old stockholm,
that the jazz guys love to serenade,
as cool as the west coast school.

i take zoot's gentle stylings into
sleep with me and, in the morning,
to my noontime swim at the ymca.

what a good friend henry is.
what good friends i have all over the country,
all over the world.

Don't Ask Us to Plan too Far Ahead

For two months I kept on my calendar
to catch Lee Konitz at the bakery,
because he's getting old,
because I am.

When the December week arrived,
the engagement had been cancelled.

I still steadfastly resist
postponements of my commitments,
often foolishly,

but I can't kid myself: the years of
chronically cancelled engagements
aren't far off—already I make fewer plans,
especially when travel and responsibilities
are involved.

Lee and I,
as we slow down,
are speeding in the fast lane towards
indefinite postponements.

ivan albright: *into the world there came a soul called ida,*
1929-30

no, there is no soul,
except perhaps as metaphor
for traits of energy that may
themselves be an illusion.

at twenty years,
at twenty days,
at twenty seconds,
for the world
the flesh is all and it
is always aging, uglifying.

eventually you can't even
bring yourself to fuck it.

the painter labored many months
to tell us,
indelibly,

memento mori, mother;
memento mori, motherfuckers.

186

a streetcar named greed

there's no more "streetcar named desire,"
just a bus now to desire street,
which was named, i learn, after the
daughter, desiree, of a rich man.

the puritans,
some men, some women,
some straight, some gay,
are once again aspiring to wean us
from our lusts.
they only drive desire underground
where sigmund freud is romping with
maria laveau.

the surface effect is a sublimation
into a raging and insatiable thirst for
money, power, criminality, and
judgement.

his mother dressed him as a girl

and foisted on him
the edifying, sentimental, feminizing literature
of the little lord fauntleroys.

he rejected her designs
for the male world of his father,
for adventure in life and literature,
for virtue in its latinate root sense
of strength,
not its corrupted one of
christian abnegation.

his religion was that of the pagans,
the pre-christian rituals of nature
upon which the christian ones were grafted,

and if, indeed, his death was a true suicide,
then both he and his father died
the deaths of noble romans,
appropriating to themselves
the final act of self-determination.

i believe that there indeed is
such a noble quality as
"the courage to be queer,"
and i applaud those who accept what they
have found to be or chose to become.

there is also, though, a courage in
the affect of the traditional,
the heterosexual,
the genetically predisposed masculine,
in resistance to the pressure of
a mother or an entire society.
i have observed it in the sons of

188

the most orthodox feminists,
determined to tame, civilize, androgenize

their offspring according to the most
rationalized and ideological of blueprints.
and some succeed, but others fail
as did the doyennes of oak park,

although they may pursue their sons,
these women in testosteronic white,
across the broad savannahs of the psyche.

no matter: struggle is good.
and if eventually it kills one,
well, it renders peace at last
more sweet.

eastern guys appreciate their wives more

they're glad their wives are attractive;
they're glad their wives are pretty;
but they don't demand that they
stay as young and flawless and cosmetic
as the movie starlets.

they appreciate that their wives are good mothers.
they like coming home to dinner
with the wife and kids.
they like doing things with the other couples
that they've known for years.
they like the idea of growing old together.

the marriage can survive an affair on either side,
if it only happens once, though they'd prefer
(for their spouse at least) that it not happen at all.

nowadays, the wives often also work.
the guys help out more at home,
spend less time, if any, in the bars.
grandkids come; grandparents age
and need to be cared for.

somehow colleges get paid for,
often catholic ones, sometimes even the ivy league
or a small liberal arts college,
if the kid can earn some scholarship money.

a comfortable retirement is a goal.
maybe an oft-postponed vacation
somewhere warm. an early retirement,
sometimes considered, would leave them
at loose ends anyway.

along the way, there are, thank god, a few series
worth watching on t.v. all the better if the local college
or nearest major league team stays competitive.

a laid-off husband or wife is the real test of
the family. more often than not, the family
pulls together, meets the challenge, and survives.

eastern guys appreciate their wives more.
maybe their wives appreciate them more.
maybe on both sides there's a lot to appreciate.
maybe the demands from both sides
are more reasonable.

you fit in eventually

everyone assumes and says i'm
probably already writing tons of
poems about these few days in
new orleans, but i haven't penned
a word until today, weeks afterwards—
i didn't even jot a note until the return
flight. i let the poems come to me these
days, confront life without literary
mediation, and don't fret about the
ones that get away.

as time goes by

i speak to strangers
all the time now,
out of the blue,
impetuously,
hesitating only momentarily,
unable to stop myself,
on planes,
at the ymca pool,
in bookstores,
crossing campus.

i ask about the food they're eating,
the wine or beer they've selected,
their destination, the weather,
the book they're reading,
life in general.

to the woman who is on the flight
back from grading
advanced placement essays
in daytona beach,
i say, of *the power and the glory*,
"that's a great book."

"unh-hunh," she says,
and goes back to her reading.

well, how was i supposed to compete
with a great book like that?

reprieve

in the hospital room
my dear friend trish,
hearing the doctor refer to a tumor,
comes to my bedside
with tears in her eyes
and takes my hand in hers.
she is virtually speechless.

i am worrying about
getting back across the country
and possibly surviving an extended sequence
of surgeries, radiation, chemo,
but i wonder at the intensity of her sympathy
even though i am greatly moved by it.

gradually i realize that she's assuming
i'll be a dead man within days.
she and her husband have been among
my closest friends since they were in
innumerable classes of mine starting in 1965.
i am close to their entire family.
of course she is distraught.

it will turn out that i don't have
any tumor at all,
let alone a malignant one.
it's just a bowel obstruction
(though those can kill you too,
and quickly, but not when immediately
treated, as this one has been).

but my will to live
has been awakened once again
for my children, my precious manuscripts,
and my best, nonpareil, friends.

My Three Sons

They are different from each other in many ways.
The first-born is a salesman;
the next, a fireman,
the youngest, a writer and teacher.
But they also have much in common.
They have all declined to hate their father.
They have all come to know
that it is a different thing to be a man
than to be a woman
and that it is a difficult thing
to be either.
They are all better husbands
than I have ever been,
and the first two, who have children,
are far better fathers than I ever was.
The third will be also.

They are all very loved by their father,
who has spent a lifetime
learning to be a father
and who is not entirely there yet.

He does not really believe in re-incarnation either,
but as he learns, always belatedly, from his mistakes,
he begins to understand why so many people
do covet those second or third or more chances.

Such a phenomenon seems less important, though,
when one's own sons do such a good job of
learning from the mistakes of their father.

Vincent Van Gogh: *The Mulberry Tree*, 1889

In the artist's words,
"It's dense yellow foliage
was of a magnificent yellow color
against a very blue sky,
in a white stony field
with sunshine from behind."

He neglected to mention that
he'd plugged the whole scene into
God's own infinitely voltaged battery.

No one was ever more alive than he.
It is not just that
he was creative:
he embodied creation…
The creator took possession of him.
Death and life were one:
both crackled with brain-music.

He may have known something
that we do not yet,
a reality defying words.

His brain exploded into galaxies.

Strong Women

In the papers delivered at the conference,
we hear a lot about "Strong Women,"
in films, on T.V., in novels, and in life.
When I was growing up, "Strong Women"
used their strength for others: husbands,
lovers, children, aging parents, their employers,
their neighbors, their church, their God, their
country, the poor, the sick, the students, et cetera.

Today, "Strong Women," are strong for themselves,
and it's considered a strong and noble act to
liberate themselves from obligations
and responsibilities to others.

It's a mindless cliché and yet it's accepted
even in intellectual circles.

Strong men are derided as "patriarchs," "macho."

My mother was a "modern" woman and was
"Strong" in the current, tyrannical sense,
but I was largely raised by the former brand
of strong women, my aunts and the nuns,
and by a man who was either strong enough
to remain with my mother for my sake,
or too weakened by the war and deprived of
alternatives by the social restraints of those
times to leave her, and me.

He performed duties towards me she had
liberated herself from, along with liberating
herself from any duties to him and from
any sweetness of disposition towards
either one of us. So death kindly
stopped for him at fifty, and I stayed
away from her for twenty years.

Second-Hand Television

I never really even minded
second-hand smoke that much,

but now I can't escape
second-hand t.v.

It's in front of every seat
on the airlines,

and on every computer,

in every bar and restaurant,

on busses and in limos,

even in the study lounges
of the universities,

and of course my wife
always has it on
for "background noise,"
in our living room,
which is also
my reading and writing and thinking
room.

In general I'm against more laws,
but if everyone else is going to agitate
for their favorite imposition
upon the personal freedoms of others,

then I want all televisions kept
farther from me than the last, lonely
cigarette.

Milestones

Except for dealing with
the multiple bureaucracies of Medicare,
I really didn't mind turning 65.

I didn't mind turning 60 either,
or 50 or 40,
although at 53 I was just about a dead man,
which is one reason I didn't mind
turning 60 or 65.

Now I reflect on so many of my betters,
who didn't make it this far
Hemingway, Faulkner, Lawrence, Hopkins, Thomas—
and on those I've personally admired
who have set goals I should aspire to:
Bukowski at 73; Edward Field still, in his eighties,
a wise but mischievous kid.
I realized I have enough things wrong with me
that I could, on any otherwise fine day,
trip over the bucket now.
But 73 is only 8 years off,
and even the eighties seem all too reachable.

But the worst of it would be having to watch
my kids grow towards death as well.

And the thought of them preceding me
into the unknown land
is simply unthinkable:
believing against unbelief,
I would have to go in search of them.

The Firmament

Descending the emergency exit stairs
(a well-kept secret)
after the stirring finale of the near-perfect production
of "Fidelio," the somewhat frumpy woman,
a step or two beneath us, turns to say,

"You can always depend on Beethoven, can't you?"
And I agree with her, even as I recall
Kevin Chu, a lifeguard at the pool,
remarking just the other day,
as he slipped *The Dark Side of the Moon,*
into his CD player,
"This one is never really the wrong choice."

And he and the old lady are both right,
and their judgments could be extended
to a few others also—Sinatra, Ella, Nat, Miles,
Cummings, Hemingway, Van Gogh, Keats, Plath—

And Thank God for these Blazing Geniuses,
who light our paths beyond the sunless craters
to a sanctuary from pedestrian cares,

and don't forget that even those
the world described and perhaps derides
as "suicides,"

are still in fact alive.

Cathedral

We walk there from the opera house,
the Disney Philharmonic Hall,
the stages for the standard repertory
and experimental dramas,
the Museum of Contemporary Art,
the expensive condos and bistros.

John Fante's Bunker Hill has not been
flattened though he wouldn't
recognize it. You tread a gentle
Golgotha to enter the cathedral,
descend the aisle to a broad, multi-
angled, postmodernistically de-
centered (or multi-centered) sanctuary,

Christ on a chickenwire cross.

The altar flat as a table,
a *mesa*,
a place to share the *masa*,
the first communion or last supper.

"Superstition" is not sneered at.
The spiritual is not supercilious.
The devotions of the people—
to the Virgin Mother, to Cesar Chavez,
are celebrated in the slanting alcoves.

It must be the cathedral most invested
with the turns of the imagination
since Cordova or Coventry.

From outside, a seeming fortress;
from within, a window onto everywhere.

Enclave and refuse,
in and out of the city,
a part of it and yet
apart from it.

The polyphonic music of the garden
mixes waterfall and freeway
traffic. A matterhorn of brown
construction dirt is visible above
the wall, a ridge away.

A *reredos* from Spain
brought to the New World,
carried north,
stored then restored to its former grandeur,
finds its new home
in our old world/new Aztlan.

Down the hill lie Chinatown,
Cinco de mayo,
Skid Row, Little Tokyo,
City Hall, the courts, the cops,
the Biltmore and the Bradbury Building,
the towers of the Bonaventure,
the convention center, Coliseum, Lakers,
flatlands, ghettos, harbors, and the sea.

Just to the north,
the Polyglot Chavez Ravine,
just to the east, the "contagious" country
hospital, just to the west: Hollywood.

And on three sides of the city, the mountains;
beyond the mountains, the vast Mojave Desert;
to the west, the sea, Micronesia, Asia.
The cynics mock the cathedral as
"The Taj Mahony,"

after the Cardinal who commissioned it.
I laugh, but pin my hopes upon it
as a place of peace.

I want to hear the echoes in it of
"O Holy Night." I hope the devil in us
doesn't blow it up.

And as for its inclusiveness,
a scrap of scripture is inscribed
on stone in many languages;

and as for gender, well, we've had for
centuries our patron saint of tomboys:
Joan of Arc (and now Joan of Arcadia).

Hart Crane shuddered like a bell tower
into elegy.

Wallace Stevens knew the steeple was
the pinnacle alike of ethics and aesthetics.

Auden sent petitions up,
embraced the ambiguities
of light and power,
came to know, with age, anxiety.

The rich can still buy their way in
(to crypt-interment anyway),

but the poor of heart
shall still see God
inherit the Cathedral
and the kingdom that will be
or not be of this earth.

Henri de Toulouse-Lautrec: *profile of a prostitute,* 1892-94

they say we know she was a whore
because her bed is left unmade.
maybe the red hair also,
but i don't know—there's something
matronly about her also:
maybe the double chin,
maybe just the morning's pre-cosmetic
dullness of complexion.

pensive? sure. who isn't on a
morning after... *after anything?*

regretful? who does not have his
or her regrets in certain moods,
at certain times of day.

a bold indictment of an exploitative
institution? yeah, well, that's what
we're supposed to say these days,
right?

and how about the ways in which the
sacrament of matrimony exploits men,
the double-cross of it,
the reasons why prostitutes and
mistresses become the havens
that they flee to?

how about the consolidation of the "official,"
with the abolition of alternatives?

"nowhere to run to, baby;
nowhere to hide."

beware monopolies.
beware all spinners of webs.

the stepford boys

the women say picasso was
a bastard and a prick.
of course what really gets their goat
is that he *was* a goat,
right down to his last gruff gasp,
never toed the line or spouted it,
didn't let his women dominate him,
was not afraid to paint them
at their worst.
they tried to lay down the law,
but he just went on laying them
and leaving them.

today we are much better men
than Pablo was.

we're strong enough to be weak.

that's why they don't call us
bastard penises:

they call us pussies.

Wedlock Sunday

she is working in the garden,
facing away from me,
trimming the bougainvillea,
still trim herself and youthful,
relaxed and free of cares,
doing something she enjoys,
something that she always has enjoyed,
and having lost all conception of
the passing of the hours,

and i feel a tenderness for her
that i may never have felt during
the selfish passion of young manhood,

and i wish the bitterness that
have more than merely punctuated
our thirty years together
could be magically obliterated
(which will never happen—let's
not kid ourselves—but perhaps for the
rest of this afternoon and evening
they will be.)

i resolve to do and say
only kindnesses to her
over dinner and in front of
the pbs mystery that we've been following

and not to react to
any sarcasms or schemes
she may slip into out of habit, hunger,
merlot, tiredness, or contemplation of
the work week's rattling hours
of third graders, parents, colleagues,
homework, grades, and art projects,

lying once again in wait for her.

Gerry's Day

it came to me today in the shower:
how much I prefer february to the other months
because it's shorter,
and that there's no good reason why
the other months could not be
just as brief as well.

we just need more of them.

with thirteen months we could fit
364 days in.
then we could have a fourteenth month
of just one day
(and two in leap years).

because for thirteen months
weeks would remain at seven days,
we'd know at the end of each week
that we were one-fourth, one-half,
or three-fourths of the way to payday,
or at the very day itself.
no more of those messy extra days
that mean we are not as close
to payday as we feel we ought to be,
those twenty-ninth and thirtieth and thirty-first
days of the month that constitute the major cause
of bounced checks and deflated celebrations.
these would be months that we could trust,
good, solid, honest, manageable months,
the kind our earliest ancestors swore by
in their caves and barrows.

it will be only fitting that
the fourteenth month
be named for me
and celebrated in my honor,

a paid holiday and payday both
(and two of them in leap year).

happy gerry's day to you;
we'll all live in a zoo;
we will all look like monkeys,
and we'll smell like them too.

Not on the Church Calendar

The vernal equinox is fast approaching,
but what many have not heard of are
the Vernal and Autumnal
festivals of the Equiballs.
These too occur in Spring and Fall,
when the title of the earth
is less severe.
It is then that a man's balls
hang equidistant towards
the center of the earth
and from his kundalini.
The celebratory dates vary considerably,
of course, from man to man,
because, as every tailor knows,
one ball or t'other
is destined to swing lower
a little or a lot.
So in some cases the torso may be
tilted at a cosmic angle no less than that
of Pisa's Tower,
while the balls hang equitably as
the scales of justice.
To each man falls twice a year
this personal holiday of
his pendulous appendices
to be celebrated, as befits these parts,
not merely without fanfare,
but, indeed, most privately.

Colonoscopy

under the kind weather
of the demerol and valium,
my eyes fixed on the monitor,
i retrace the inner, fundamental
passage up the alimentary canal,
a latter-day balso snell,
but with less murky landscape
thanks to laxatives and fasting
than the trenches of holland or venice,
england or l.a. it is a twisting journey
similar to many i've awakened from.
the flesh is pulsing, muscular, red—
just as i'd imagine coronary chambers
or a whole series of vaginas
(have fun with that one, Sigmund).
look at those little seeds the eggplant left,
unflushed by the gallon of the polyethylene wash,
with its sense memory of castor oil or crank cases.
we will not speculate upon those cloudy pools—
no polyps peeping out of crevices, though,
and no moray eels or japanimation octopi.

as ordered, i roll a little this way, that way
on my side; the nurse leans heavily upon
my abdomen under the orchestration of
the gastroenterologist. he comforts me with how
close to the final turn we are, and then, that we're
withdrawing now, a painless retreat from where i
hope to never have to go again,
that little shop of horrors,
mucousy and masticating inverse mouth,
that throat of anti-masculinity,
that literalized heart of darkness,
eternal realm of mistah kurtz

who outlives conrad, eliot, cormac mccarthy.
as always i just want to be released
to go back home,
recaffeinate and vegetate in front of a
less psychedelic, jugular, and Jungian
t.v.

i want to see my kids;
i want to put my works in order;
i want a few more years
in the fresh air.

Diane Arbus: *42nd Street Movie Theatre Audience*

our movie parlours were
steep as ski runs also.
often we weren't there for
the movie anyway, but for the
girl that we were with or for
where we wanted to go in the
cinema within our own skulls.

i never really managed to convince myself
the girl i was with could actually want me to
try to kiss her. even now i'm pretty sure
a lot of them were glad i didn't
and only a couple
wished i had.

and where i went
in my own head
is where i am
right at this moment.

Cézanne: The Artist's Father

Joachim Pissarro points out
that *l'evenement,* the liberal rag
the artist's dad is reading,
is where Zola had defended
the paintings of the impressionists as works,
as the productions of "serious workers,"
in a Marxist sense,
whose work had as much true
economic, social, ideological,
and humane/progressive value
as the efforts of any of the other members
of the working class.

And I would agree with the truth of that
for Cézanne and Monet and Manet and Degas
and Van Gogh and just about any of the artists
whose names have endured long enough
to spring to mind,
but I sure know plenty of self-appointed artists
and, worse, poets, of our own time
whose "work" is of value only to themselves...
No, wait, they may in fact just be wasting
their entire lifetimes when they could be doing
something, anything, that they are better at,
just as I gave up the piano for drinking.

And I tend to agree with the steam-plant welders
whom I used to drink with at the 49ers Tavern
near the university:
"Locklin," they would chorus, whenever I would
lament essay grading or committee meetings,
or the lack of respect accorded the contemporary poet,
"You've never done an honest day's work in
your life."

The Ungrateful Dead

i would imagine
most of them are.

For Henry Denander

I just read your poems
in Nerve Cowboy, 21, Spring 2006,
and noticed that you are now writing
better poems than most of the poems
that I am writing.

It's a good thing
because not too many are,

although a lot are writing poems
just as good as most of mine,

but, shit, even I can do that.

Madonna and Child, Sculpture, Italy, 1125-1150

Here the child is not merely
the Father of the Man—
the Child *is* the Man.

The Crucifixion is contained
within the Creche;
the Resurrection,
a promise in the distant future.

Redeem Mankind?
Yeah, sure.
Yeah, maybe.
Yeah, you and what army,
kid?

A Man acquainted with sorrows, indeed.
A Mother destined never to know
unalloyed maternal joy.

(Then again what mother ever has?)

(The father/stepfather is, as usual,
left out of the equation.
always a bit player.
Often played for a fool.)

Vanessa Bell: *Charleston Garden,* 1933

the woman garbed in rose
sews a lily garment
draped across her lap.
the sun breaks through the ample foliage
that lines the pathway to the formless door.
even the impressionistic sky/sea upholstery
of the chair the woman sits on
is a work of art.
everything about the place is.
vanessa, clive, and duncan
excelled in the decorative,
the arts of civilized living,
the apotheosis of the unnecessary.

we spent five weeks in the summer of 1993
in england and wales. i battled pulmonary
emboli from heathrow back to heathrow.
my son and i killed time in the garden,
while my wife and daughter viewed the
artifacts inside the cottage. we tossed
pebbles in the stream. we yawned and
sweated and rehydrated. i remember
the long lane on and off the property.

i battled my wife too, but—sorry, ladies—
didn't batter her. i could barely make it up
the hills and endless staircases. temporarily
the exercise helped, though. the spirits and
the ales helped even more.

within six weeks i'd be in intensive care in
California, my drinking days already melting
to nostalgia, then indifference.

my wife would love to be the woman in this
painting, with her life of arts and crafts and
living but inhuman things.
she's read a tower of books about
bloomsbury, and remembers them. she can
even keep straight their genealogy of morals,
the entanglements, arrangements, and paternities,
that always fail me in my literature classes,
as futile as teaching *lie* and *lay*.

i'll never be able to give her charleston farm,
not to mention sissinghurst or knole, but
she's turned our modest home into a poor man's
(woman's) monk's house, and made me nod assent
to the possibility of a return,
five years from now, when she retires,
to england and to wales (where I taught a term
in 1989: we lived in a menai bridge and gazed
across the straights at bangor and snowdonia).
i'm not sure what her feelings are towards
the more virile ireland and scotland.

and i'm afraid i may be fool enough to do it.

Good in Bed

I don't understand why guys worry about
whether they are ranked good or bad in bed
by the ladies who presume to
adjudicate such performances.
After all the very fact that they're talking about you
indicates something is commanding their sexual interest.
furthermore, if any woman ever claimed
that *I* were less than excellent in bed,
I'd know that it must be *her fault,*
not only because,
as the terpsichorean proverb observes,
it takes a minimum of two to tango,
but, definitively, because I can testify
from personal experience,
that I have always been
sensational even when in bed
only with myself.

219

Pierre Auguste Renoir

before i'd hang one of his
florid ladies on my wall,
i'd hang myself there,

but i'd let him buy
me lunch.

Why I Didn't Make the Rounds

When I quit drinking I thought I would
keep up my bar life anyway.
It has been my social life for thirty years.
Most of my friends were there.
Everyone knew where they could find me.
I never entertained at home.
It was a refuge when things were bad at home.
I was at ease with the traditional
masculinity of life.

At first, I hit a few,
but given the circulatory problems in my legs,
I was not even physically comfortable
on a barstool or at a low table anymore.
And so much of the talk now seemed
just the alcohol talking.
The bar women were not aging well.
And none of the things
that had seemed so important—pool, foosball,
televised sports, liar's poker, arm wrestling,
political disputation, the occasional squaring off,
seemed all that important anymore.

The booze had facilitated
the friendship and sex,
but I couldn't reach for the vodka-tonic anymore—
I had decided not to die yet,
the kids and students and manuscripts
that still might need me.
And so I had no compelling reasons
to seek out the bars anymore,
not even when on the road—I already knew
they weren't much fun without intoxication.

God Needs More Churches

Toad glances at the passenger seat
and asks Mrs. Toad:

"Have we ever passed a Second Baptist Church?"
"No, only the First ones—about one per town."

"How about the Crystal Methodists?"
"Ha! That's a good one."

"The Holy Bowlers?"
"You're on a roll, Toad."

"The Young Presbyterians?"
"I don't get it."
"*Presbyterians* means *Elders*."
"You're stretching it."

"Roman(tic) Catholic...
Episcopapists...
The Y'Amish?"

"Good roots."

"Okay, the truth is I did see
a Fourth Lutheran Church once.
You were raised Missouri Synod, weren't you?"

"Yes...what were the first three like?"

"Somebody had burned them down."

"Who would have done that?"

"I just assumed it had been done by *you*."

Can't Buy You Love

Thanks to being born
into a working-class family
at the start of World War II,

and to, as an adult, perfecting
a propensity for wine, women, and song.
Toad periodically experienced
something very close to dire poverty,
and, in spite of a Scottish thriftiness,
in expenditures upon the mere necessities,
he was never very securely removed
from a life upon the streets.

On the other hand,
Toad not only did at least
HAVE a life,

but what a fucking life
he had!

I Hate Hollywood

I hate its blockbusters.
I hate its expensive blockbuster theaters.
I hate its parking problems.
I hate its potholes.
I hate its drug dealers, and
I hate their customers.
I hate its gang mentality.
I hate its rip-off apartments and motels and restaurants.
I hate its clubs, but I love its cemeteries.
I hate its lack of loyalty, and
I hate its rip-off royalties.
I hate the way its kids are raised.
I hate everything old about it, and
I hate everything new.
I hate the way everyone votes
for the same people,
and then votes to recall them.
I hate its celebrities who try to be poets, and
I hate its poets who aspire to be celebrities.
I hate its hypocrisies, and
I hate its theocracies.
I hate everything Fitzgerald, Faulkner,
West, and Hemingway hated about it.
I hate what it did or tried to do to Bukowski.
I hate its ersatz Bukowskians.
I hate the Hollywood Sign, the Hollywood Bowl,
The Hollywood Bowling Alleys, the Hollywood
Hills and Hollywood Canyons, and
I do not discriminate in my hatred of all
its residents of any race, and all its tourists
who stare at the Chinese Theater, and I hate
the homeless who mug them and murder them,
but I applaud that they burn down each other's
homes and businesses and flatten each other's
tires. I even hate things that are non-existent,

such as its entire infrastructure, whose pipes burst
every day because they didn't have a dollar spent
on them in 100 delusional years.
Obviously, I don't hate its earthquakes.
I don't hate Ed Ruscha's painting of a
Hollywood sunset, behind a Hollywood sign,
which means the sun is somehow setting in the north,
I don't hate Randy Newman because if you read
between the lines he hates Los Angeles, also.
I hate those foolish drivers who lead police
on car chases and then are surprised when
they are rewarded with cracked skulls.
I have adrenal glands also, lots of them.

Maybe I should admit that Hollywood seduced
the love of my life away from me,
but I am too sophisticated,
as you can see, to allow
that to jaundice
my urbane appraisal of
the Woods of Holly.

Thumbnail Guide for the Senior Couplers

No matter how you coupled,
if you coupled at all,
and if it was fun while you were doing it,
and you came (or close) at the end of it,
who cares who was putting what into whom,
where, or how many times?

These and many other details are INESSENTIAL!!!
Maybe it was just a damn fine backrub!!!
It's not even ESSENTIAL that there be a next time.
It's more ESSENTIAL that you retain a memory
OF THIS TIME…and even a SENSE MEMORY
OF SOMETHING HAVING HAPPENED
will suffice.

As far as the next time is concerned,
well, you've earned a next time,
but then again, we don't always get to cash
our final pension checks in either.

And anyway, was there ever a time in our lives
when, man or woman,
LGBT or straight, we knew for sure
where our next piece of ass was coming from,
or even IF one was? And, as anyone will tell you:
the worst piece of ass you ever had,
was probably not all THAT BAD either!
And who knows, maybe we take our memories with us,
except up there, they're not just dreams, they're
like a porno film in which we star eternally,
and God's a smiling, ageless popcorn popping
pharmacist, distributing these little blue pills.

timing is everything

the horoscope this morning
really put me on my guard,
sent the adrenaline coursing
through my veins,
as it predicted a crucial confrontation
that would require all the will and
ingenuity that i could muster ...
until i remembered i was looking at
a week-old student newspaper.

Olfactory Poetics

As soon as I get a whiff
of "poetry" in a poem
(not excluding my own),

I strongly suspect
it isn't one.

No Free Lunch

The cat on the back of the sofa
watching the birds and squirrels
feed and frolic on the patio
outside the sliding glass window,
realizes he is living his life
in a cage
only slightly larger than that
of the parakeet.

Courtesy of his loving (themselves) owners,
who have bought his freedom
from the pet shop or pound,
he has been further relieved of the burdens
of procreation and child-rearing,
while being afforded a waived tuition
into what Buñuel nailed as
The Discreet Charms of the Bourgeoisie.

the common reader

an editor sends back
some poems of mine,
says he'd rather have some
for "the common man."

i know what he means:
he'd rather have some from
my drinking days than ones that
contemplate and spring from
works of art.

yet, i know i'm nothing if not
common, now as in the past,
and i wonder why the worker must
be seen as relegated to the barroom,
the ennui that has been made of
sports on television, the commercial
interruptions, marketing research,
the bloat of coors and bud.

do we have so low an opinion
of the common man that we assume
he is not capable of appreciating
aaron copeland, john cage, mahler,
hopper and van gogh.
poets other than bukowski,
rabbit angstrom,
death of a salesman,
stranger than paradise?

my friend, your heart is in
the right place but i think you
underrate the human potential.
when i lived in the bars, the
guys from the steam plant read
my chapbooks, passed them

around. sometimes came to
readings, sometimes still do,

and yeah, some of my poems
from those days celebrated pool
and pickled eggs, beef jerky and
baseball games, as well they should
have, but not all of them: others
dealt with honor, death, betrayal,
the verismo tragicomedy.

the common man of my day
has either died or is like me.
i think that he still understands my poems,
or could, if you'd give him the chance.
(if he looks up *verismo* it may lead him to
pagliacci and *cavalleria rusticana*—
check out *godfather three*.)

the common man of your age
is in college.

Matisse: *Le Bonheur de Vivre*, 1905-06

The colors make each other move,
upon the retinas, within the synapses.
The people are caught as absences,
photographic negatives within the
spectral flames. They are naked
as the supernatural. If Dante were
a Fauvist, this is how he would have
crayoned the afterlife. The title
is pleonastic as plasticity: To live
is to be happy, because to be alive,
in this life, is itself a happiness.

And those who are not happy
die. But that is for another
canvas altogether, one of Munch's
perhaps, or Francis (that pig) Bacon's,
or Lucien Freud's. In this Matisse,
and even in quick brushstrokes
of Van Gogh, which persist within
a corner of Matisse, the best death
is a visionary aneurism.

albrecht dürer: *adam and eve*, 1504

she has a face that would stop
a serpent in its serpentine tracks.
in fact, she has a beak on her
that strongly resembles that of
the bird on adam's branch.
she'd have to be the only lay
in town to stand a chance of
getting me to taste a fruit
that's already been in a snake's mouth.

and as if it weren't going to be
punishment enough for adam,
in exile with her somewhere east
of eden, and no flags yet invented
to pull over her head and fuck for
old glory.

it looks to me as if
the fig leaf he's selected for
this crucial day's attire

may be poison ivy.

My Fifteen Seconds of Fame

When I was much younger
and had a big black beard
and long black hair,
if I went to Tijuana,
I heard, "Hey, Fidel!"

And at the Top Dog in Berkeley,
someone would call, "I know you—you're
Jerry Garcia!"

And once at a hamburger stand
off Highway One in Lucia,
a woman called me
The Illegitmate Son of Mr. Madman
(which became a chapbook of mine
from Slipstream Press),

so I think it can be forgiven,
now that I'm in my seventies,
if someone on the street will occasionally
ask me, "Aren't you Gerry Locklin?"

And it will occur to me that,
for what it's worth,
I actually am.

the silence

in *rituals,* by cees noteboom,
a character speaks of the "wonderful silence"
that a nuclear catastrophe would bring.

no one in truth desires that,
but i can understand
the longing inspired by the concept.

it's new year's but i don't
turn on the rose bowl yet.
i don't turn on the countdown
of the greatest jazz hits
on the greatest jazz station,
KLON.
even this writing is a sort of inner noise
not altogether joyful.

solitary confinement is one of the hells;
the voices of the schizophrenic are another.

i cherish this hour
in a deafened cosmos of the mind,
but only for as long
as i am not condemned to it.

at midnight

at midnight, i look up
from the gilberto sorrentino book
that i've been reading under flashlight

and i notice that the dipper and north star
have moved across the sky

and for the first time in my life
i *feel* the fact that i am in motion
that everything is,
and simultaneously for the first time in my life
i do not want to die,
i remember how sad for years it left my daughter
when her grandfather died,

and i don't want to leave her with
a second sadness,
and for the first time in my life
i understand why anyone would want
to believe in reincarnation,
and would want to come back
to this world.

ACKNOWLEDGEMENTS

Thank you to the editors of the following books and chapbooks from which many of these poems were taken as well as to the editors of the dozens of magazines that originally published many of these poems. Apologies to any book publishers that may have been unintentionally omitted.

Sunset Beach, Hors Commerce Press, 1967
Star Trek & Such, The Wormwood Review Press, 1968
Toad Poems, Runcible Spoon, 1970
Poop and Other Poems, MAG Press, 1972
Son of Toad, The Wormwood Review Press, 1973
Son of Poop, MAG Press, 1973
The Criminal Mentality, Red Hill Press, 1976
Pronouncing Borges, The Wormwood Review Press, 1977
2 Summer Sequences, Maelstrom Press, 1979
Some Toad Songs, The Wormwood Review Press, 1979
Two Weeks on Mr. Stanford's Farm, Rumba Train Press, 1980
Two for the Seesaw and One for the Road, Northwoods Press, 1980
A Clear & Present Danger to Society, Four Zoas Night House Press, 1981
Scenes from a Second Adolescence, Applezaba Press, 1981
The Women Have Won, Wormwood Review Press, 1982
The Death of Jean-Paul Sartre and Other Poems, Ghost Pony Press, 1987
Children of a Lesser Demagogue, The Wormwood Review Press, 1987
A Constituency of Dunces, Slipstream Publications, 1988
On the Rack, Trout Creek Press, 1988
The Treasure of the Sierra Faulkner, Zerx Press, 1989
The Rochester Trip, Vergin' Press, 1990
The Illegitimate Son of Mr. Madman, Slipstream Publications, 1991
A Yank at Bangor: Poems from the Welsh Teaching Experience,
   Vergin'Press, 1991
The Firebird Poems, Event Horizon Press, 1992
Toad Writes Short Stories, BSG Press, 1993
The Bard of Amphibia, The Wormwood Review Press, 1994
The Cabo Conference, Proper PH Publications, 1995
A Sure Bet, Water Row Press, 1996

The New Male, Bleeding Heart Press, 1995
The Last Round-Up, Wormwood Review Press, 1996
Art Farmer Suite & Other Poems, Zerx Press, 1997
The Active Ingredient & Other Poems, Liquid Paper Press, 1997
Go West Young Toad: Selected Writings, Water Row Press, 1998
The Hospital Poems, Kings Estate Press, 1998
The Back East Poems, Liquid Paper Press, 1999
This Sporting Life and Other Poems, JVC Books, 1999
Running into Ger, Royal Vagrant Press, 1999
Hemingway Colloquium: The Poet Goes to Cuba, Event Horizon Press, 1999
The Face of Chet Baker, Zerx Press, 1999
The Iceberg Theory and Other Poems, Lummox Press, 2000
Familiarities, Lummox Press, 2001
The Mystical Exercycle, The Chuckwagon, 2002
The Life Force Poems, Water Row Press, 2002
The Author's Not Quite Dead Yet, Showerhead Press, 2002
The Dorset Poems, Bottle of Smoke, 2003
Henry's Gift and Other Poems, Pariah Press, 2003
The Modigliani/Montparnasse Poems, dOOm-AH Books, 2003
The Ultimate Pessimist & Other Poems, Pitch Fork Press, 2003
The Spirit of the Struggle: Jazz Poems 2005, Zerx Press, 2006
New Orleans, Chicago, and Points Elsewhere, R)V Press, 2006
The Cézanne/Pissarro Poems, World Parade Books, 2007
the ristorante godot, Bottle of Smoke Press, 2007
Gerald Locklin: New & Selected Poems, World Parade Books, 2008
Wedlock Sunday and Other Poems, Liquid Paper Press, 2007
The Plot of Il Travatore and Other Poems, Kamini Press, 2008
Modest Aspirations, Lummox Press, 2010
You Need Never Look Out a Window: The Complete Coagula Poems Volume 1,
   Flechaverde Inc., 2011
Deep Meanings: Selected Poems 2008-2013, Presa Press, 2013
*This Marriage of Man the Maker and Mother Nature: The Complete Coagula
   Poems Volume II,* Coagula Publications, 2014
Poets and Pleasure Seekers: New and Selected Poems 2010-2015, Spout Hill
   Press, 2015

Thank you especially to David and Patricia Cherin for supporting me in this project and granting me permission to the works and to Raymond Hammond and all at NYQ Books for publishing this collection. I'd also like to thank Zachary Locklin, Fred Voss, Jeff Epley, Sean Casey, Dave Newman, Ray Zepeda, Donna Hilbert, Henry Denander, Michael Hathaway, Keith Milo, and always, Diliana Stamatova.

I'd also like to give a very special thank you and shout out to Mark Weber and Michael Basinski, whose extensive bibliographies of Gerry's work helped solved many mysteries and free up many many hours of my time.

Always a generous person, Gerry once wrote a blurb for my first book of poems, in which he said, "The next time a blurb is called for, I suspect it will be I who is petitioning him for it. And it had damn well better be a glowing one!"

Well, Gerry, how did I do?

Gerald Locklin (1941-2021) was born in Rochester, NY. A prolific writer of both poetry and prose, he published over a hundred books in his lifetime, including *The Firebird Poems* (Event Horizon Press), *Go West, Young Toad* (Water Row Books), *Charles Bukowski: A Sure Bet* (Water Row Books), and *Down and Out* (Event Horizon Press). The Oxford Companion to Twentieth Century Literature in the English Language calls him "a central figure in the vitality of Los Angeles writing." From 1965-2007, he was professor of English at California State University, Long Beach. He lived in Long Beach, CA.

Clint Margrave is the author of several books, including the novel *Lying Bastard* (Run-Amok Books) and three poetry collections, *Salute the Wreckage, The Early Death of Men,* and most recently, *Visitor,* all from NYQ Books. He lives in Long Beach, CA.

Printed in the USA
CPSIA information can be obtained
at www.ICGtesting.com
LVHW042314300124
770397LV00013B/31